JUDE ADAMS

The Window to My Soul

A Memoir of Sorts

First published in 2019 by Jude Adams

Typeset by Parkers Design and Print Ltd.
Printed and bound by Parkers Design and Print Ltd, Canterbury, CT1 3PP

ISBN 978-1-9160473-0-3

A CIP record for this book is available from the British Library.

Contents

Introduction

"Writing comes from the most secret recesses."
– V.S. Naipal

W hy do we write memoirs? To have our voices heard? To have people pay attention to us? Perhaps because we want to write a book and starting with our own story is an obvious place to begin.

I had always remembered very fondly a birthday present sent to me by my godfather in Canada in the 1960s. Four LPs telling the story of *Alice in Wonderland* with the book inserted into the base of the box – a prototype boxset. That concept of combining the audio and the visual as a physical product appealed to me. Real lives have always fascinated me, I have always been an avid reader of biographies and memoirs, and I felt that writing a memoir was what I wanted to do.

Writing about yourself and your life is not easy. I thought that perhaps it might appear arrogant, a form of therapy session, naval gazing. It is none of those things. Perhaps it is all of those things and more. I chose to write a "memoir of sorts" because it did feel like a kinder option, both to myself and the reader, than an autobiography or a more conventional memoir. A vehicle for telling stories from my life, telling tales, writing poetry and turning my hand to something visual too. A creative mashup. A book that is both of substance and beautiful to look at. Presented in an understated coffee table format, a book to be dipped into, absorbed, reflected upon and relished, or just read from start to finish.

Rather than a standard linear narrative, *The Window to My Soul* floats across my lifetime, stopping to dive into episodes that I believe have shaped me. And I chose to combine it with an album of songs triggered by the contents of the book. Same title. Same artwork. At once interwoven but standing alone in a similar way to my *Alice in Wonderland* box set.

It has been hard at times. During those times, I was sorely tempted to fly off into my imagination and make something up. Far easier sometimes to write about the land of make believe. But I resisted the temptation.

I have had thoughts, often late at night, that I should turn the light on and write those thoughts down. How I might change what I've said. What I've written. But in doing that this pursuit would be endless. At some stage you have to decide that it is finished. For now I have finished.

I have endeavoured not to share any myths nor self-deception. To ensure that the stories I tell are told with a genuine belief that they are my memories.

"Like many people as we get older, we forget the majority of things,
but not the things that matter to us." – *Ann Atkins*

This book contains things that matter to me.

Definitions

"Memoir isn't the summary of a life; it's a window into a life, very much like a photograph in its selective composition. It may look like a casual and even random calling up of bygone events. It's not; it's a deliberate construction."
– *William Zinsser, On Writing Well (30th anniversary edition)*

"Writers are more important than heads of state."
– *Nawal El Saadawi*

"A good memory is the one you can give away."
– *Billy Connolly*

"Writers and comedians are magpies. They pick things up and transform them."
– *Val McDermid*

"I would say now ... I don't how to write. I don't know how I wrote or how I will write. I don't know how to do it, I'm not sure I know. There is that thing where you go, how did I ever do any of that and will I be able to do it again."
– *Conor MacPherson (playwright and writer)*

"I think the moment you think you know how to do it the writing sort of dies cos it all becomes craft and you've done it a million times and it all becomes mechanical."
– *Hossein Amini (screenwriter)*

"Stories are like a window to the soul of the teller."
– *Graham Norton*

"A memoir is how someone remembers one's own life."
– *Gore Vidal*

memoir
/ˈmɛmwɑː/

noun

1. a historical account or biography written from personal knowledge.
"in 1924 she published a short memoir of her husband"
synonyms: account, historical account, history, record, chronicle, annal(s), commentary, narrative, story, report, portrayal, depiction, sketch, portrait, life, life story, profile, biography
(Google)

Travel

Introduction

I sit at my desk. The Wimbledon Tennis Championships is playing softly downstairs on the radio as I reflect on a weekend at a music festival in the searing heat, packed in with thousands of other people – literally the great unwashed. I am overtired from driving and sleeping for 6 nights in a rather fabulous but cramped 44-year-old reconditioned VW camper van called Flo. My head is almost permanently stuck at an angle from either standing or sleeping in a cramped space and I have arthritic sensations in my fingers from the force with which it took to simply turn the steering wheel.

Emotional still, from trying to have a conversation with my bank that felt more like an interrogation: "As you've forgotten your login details, Madam, I will need to ask you some further security questions." I managed my address, middle names and birth month. "Can you tell me if you have an overdraft facility and how much it might be and can you tell me what your mortgage was when you set up the account?" "That was 20 years ago," I reply, astonished. "My partner tends to deal with things like this, so I'm sorry but I'll have to call you back." I feel pathetic and reach for a tissue.

Then half an hour later I post joyous photographs on Facebook showing our fun-filled weekend when in reality I found the heat, the crowds, the trek into the festival arena and the quality of some of the acts exhausting. But great company, conversation and humour was to be found in our gang of four. Flo too had become a special friend but perhaps the fondest memory of all, and for us a first, was our own portable flushing loo.

It became apparent when I met my wife Marg in 1995, that travel was likely to be high on her agenda and it was she who threw music festivals into the mix. With local friends, the Brixton Belles, we went regularly to WOMAD. On the first of those forays, as a virgin festival goer, I managed to get separated from Marg before I'd even picked up my ticket. I didn't feel lost, although in a way I was. Feeling lost can be scary. Panic can set in. I once got lost in a car park at the Uttoxeter races when I was a young teenager. Ever since then, a slight shudder of panic sets in if I sense that I am lost. The relief at feeling found again is utterly wonderful. Finding Marg again when I thought I'd lost her at WOMAD was wonderful too. She may have been more concerned at my going off with her credit card with no means of communication, but it was also the dawning for both of us as to how much we meant to each other.

There in the sun-drenched fields, some of us would adorn ourselves in leopard print sarongs and Chanel. When those fields on the banks of the Thames became rain-soaked, we employed the services of some kind souls in our party to go out and forage for pies for twelve, as we attempted to squash into the front room of our bungalow – a 1970s retro tent, which was our chosen camping option then. We later moved on to a belle tent complete with rugs, potted plants and matching accessories. Before the dawning of campervans. Portable flushing loos had not even been invented then.

Eventually, dangerously located sarsaparilla sellers, heavy-handed cannabis policing, heat exhaustion and the rapidly swelling population at this event got the better of us and a smaller band of our number defected for several years afterwards to the rather more tranquil Larmer Tree Festival. There we enjoyed much mirth and merriment, force 10 gales and fights with leaking water carriers, spilt red wine and cream silk long johns ripped in embarrassing places. Eventually people dropped off, until attendance there too was temporarily suspended.

Over the weekend at the festival in Flo, Marg had excitedly started planning a European tour. In a camper van. To take place in the next few years when she would be able to take time off or retire. Our friends and I joined in with her enthusiasm, but nervously. By the end of the second day, the trip had been mapped out. I am expecting red flags with dates on them to appear on our globe in the study in the coming week. One of our compound friends was concerned about our budgeting but Marg is, after all, a spreadsheet queen, an accountant by profession, and therefore sleep should not be lost over such matters. Great thought will be given to them, but for now I am content to let her dreams flow. My loss of sleep was possibly more likely due to a subconscious terror, that given my condition after only 1 week, I was going to be subjected to a whole year cavorting around in a tin on wheels with only intermittent periods spent on dry land.

All of this reminds me of a book that I am in the process of reading, *Travels with Myself and Another: Five Journeys from Hell* by Martha Gelhorn, in which she writes: "The only aspect of our travels that is guaranteed to hold an audience is disaster." Well, I hope that what follows in the tales of my travels isn't all disaster, but I will endeavour to share some of my more colourful moments. A little like travel photographs, which I personally find endearing and interesting, I would generally agree with Martha that most people don't. "It takes real stamina to travel," she says. It also takes quite a lot to share an enthusiasm for the travelling exploits of other people.

Which brings me to some questions. Why do we do this to ourselves? Why do we travel? Adventure. Exploration. Curiosity. Challenge. Indulging the senses with the sights, smells, tastes, sounds of a different land or location. Because we need a break. Because we believe it will do us good. For escapism. For inspiration. To get in touch with our emotions and where we are in life. For simple pleasures. Allowing us the chance to put our lives into perspective. To plot and plan. Punishment. Martha would probably suggest self-flagellation. For me, all of those things have applied at different times.

Sourcing and arranging foreign and domestic holidays has of course become easier with the advent of the internet. Travel has become, in many cases, cheaper and certainly more accessible and there is so much more variety at our fingertips. We can all be more independent in our organisation rather than relying upon travel agents. And in so doing we can easily seek out different climates, experiencing the sun on our backs when it can't be found at home, and snow when we haven't seen more than a dusting for many years. Experimenting with different foods and ways of life. Learning new languages, although I confess that this hasn't tended to be a driving force for me. Staying in unusual and unique places far and wide. Hotels, self-catering apartments and houses, yurts, huts in forest glades, beachside shacks. Delving into the history of a country or city, its customs, culture, religions.

I do feel privileged to have been able to travel to as many places as I have. I do perhaps have a regret that I have never actually lived in another country for longer than a couple of months, which perhaps in time I will be able to set straight. But I have enjoyed many wonderful holidays abroad and closer to home. Have travelled to foreign parts with family, with friends, with partners, on my own and with groups of people completely unknown to me. I have laughed, I have cried and, not speaking any foreign language to any degree worthy of note, I have gesticulated wildly. I have avoided situations and experiences because on occasions, I haven't had the energy to confront them. I have endured illness and injury, great highs and lows, whilst apparently enjoying these moments.

Over the years I would have a competition with my mum. We would look at her globe and reel off the different places we had been to. "I actually think I may have overtaken you, Mum," I proudly proclaimed, more than once on totting up the different countries we had both visited. "I can't believe that," she exclaimed. "When did that happen? Where have you been that I haven't?" Her reply is one of amazement and not a little bit of gamesmanship – something we both perhaps inherited from her father. All good fun and good-natured banter that occurred as I evolved from child into adulthood. But quietly, in her old age, I think she probably did wonder about all the places I had been to and considered how many of those adventures we hadn't shared either in person or conversation. I had certainly overtaken her when we last had such a chat. But she did well and I may always remain rather envious of the journey she made with her parents in 1949. That was a voyage on the *Queen Mary* to New York, and then on to Fort Lauderdale to stay with my great uncle. Pearls and satin dresses abound in the photographs. Grandeur and style that has long been lost and that I won't have the chance to experience.

Travel

Spanish Odysses

I t feels fitting to talk now about my first foreign trip when, as a 5-year-old, Mum and I together with the whole family, flew to Marbella in Spain. Malaga airport was our first stop. In fact, the matriarchs of the families had flown ahead to prepare the villa we had rented. That left my father, "Uncle" a family friend, his daughter, myself and my two sisters to follow on. For some reason, I wasn't fed on the flight and when I got into the airport, I was sick over a sizeable area of the terminal floor. I have a very clear memory of "Uncle" somehow producing a box of Kleenex tissues to clean me and the floor. The rest of the holiday passed without incident in a rather idyllic, and at the time for Marbella, unspoilt spot, overlooking the beach. Sindy doll weddings, buckets and spades filled our days. And the first pair of shoes that I was to fall in love with were purchased.

One of the many reasons we travel, pointed its finger at me in a tempting way in 2014. Having become transfixed on a TV series about Jewish history in Europe, most especially Córdoba in southern Spain, I decided I had to go. Forgive me for flagging up that my health was really very poor then. Myalgic Encephalomyelitis (M.E.) has taken up a significant period of time in my life and whilst it doesn't define me, it has greatly influenced me and who I now am. Whilst given a choice, I would rather it hadn't happened to me, its impact has, however, not always had negative outcomes. As a song from one of my favourite films *Chitty Chitty Bang Bang* says, "From the ashes of disaster grow the roses of success."

Why did I want to go to Córdoba so much? The answer is that I wanted to find out more about what I had seen and heard on TV and to witness the city and its treasures and history for myself. I had never been to a foreign country on my own. Was now the time to start? I didn't speak Spanish. Was that going to matter that much? It was going to be quite a long, drawn out journey. This would be quite a challenge and, in many ways, was not the best of choices for someone in my condition. But I booked a long weekend. And went. To add to the challenges, I had my phone stolen on the journey out. This triggered extreme stress levels which in turn resulted in extreme fatigue and other physical symptoms. (Before those with experience of M.E. stand up and object, I should say that this isn't always necessarily how M.E. works. There are as likely to be physical symptoms without stress to trigger them, it just makes it worse.) The impact of that outward journey meant that I was too exhausted to turn around and travel straight home and was forced to stay a full week. Far more realistic, as well as a real treat, this allowed me time to recover and to really get underneath the city, to try out my limited Spanish and wallow not only in the Jewish history and places of interest but several of the local hammams too. I returned home feeling enormously and unexpectedly empowered. I had ticked off many firsts and had confronted many fears. It was a very, very hard week at times but very enlightening, liberating and really transformational.

Which brings me finally to my 2018: A Spanish Odyssey. I am not going to write chapter and verse about the time I spent, mainly on my own, in Cadiz for 5 weeks, after which I travelled from Seville, to Córdoba again and to Granada with Marg. Rather I will share some words and a diary entry that came at the end of my time there.

"What do I think of when I think of Cadiz set at the tip
of the south-western point of Spain?"

I think of understated charm. Of café con leche sipped slowly in one of my three favourite cafés often accompanied by a buttery, crispy croissant. Of olives and beer. Paella, sunshine, blue skies, good cheer. The finest tuna to ever grace our tongues. Orange trees, old fashioned street lamps, cobbles underfoot. The gentle strum of a Spanish guitar. The soft hum of voices. Not sirens and cars. Narrow streets meandering like a maze. Tree filled squares and fountains. Archways, pillars, mosaic tiles, soft hues of ochre, terracotta, creams, pinks and blues. A melting pot of history. Of Christian, Muslim, Jew. Reflected in mosques, Cathedrals, synagogues too.

Sizzling gambas. Anchovies. Flamenco. A crazy festival with singing groups who can sing. Madness, masks and laughter. Sunshine streaming through the windows of my nest up above the roof tops where washing lines blow in the breeze. And aerials. A lot of aerials. Ornate facades adorning the faces of buildings. The crash of a wave on shore. Or a millpond facing North. I kind of fell in love with Cadiz. And then it was time to leave.

The Leaving of Cadiz.

And so today I leave Cadiz. This place has been kind to me. For 5 weeks.

When I came out, it was with a combination of excitement, hesitation, reticence. Wondering what my time here would bring. Believing that at times, I would wonder why I was here at all. That I may need to remind myself. That I would be alone in a country without knowing its language, familiar with, but not used to, its customs.

Marg had said, in response to my concerns that it may be considered an indulgence by others, "Just tell them that you can." A multitude of meanings therein. But chief amongst them that I am able to and well enough to as I emerge from my M.E..

One of the reasons for doing this was for health. Yes, I am probably 95 per cent recovered from M.E. but a year ago my GP also diagnosed seasonal affective disorder (SAD), something that had affected me greatly over the last two winters. Perhaps partly connected to M.E., to my personal make up, but also to stressful circumstances that have been presented to me over the last 3 years that have doubtless contributed and exacerbated any predisposition.

I wanted to go away to somewhere sunny but not too far, somewhere with brightness and light but not excessive heat. Another reason for my going was so I could write, to open up creative outlets that have become suppressed, swamped and somewhat dormant over the last year or two. And those floodgates have thankfully now been well and truly opened again.

I am grateful for this opportunity on so many levels. I have relished the solitude, the charm of this city, the kindness of its people, the sunshine.

Now it is time to go. Onwards into the last 2 weeks of my 2018: A Spanish Odyssey with my soulmate, partner in crime and life to explore other pearls of Andalucia.

"Adios Amigos."

Your eyes are the window,
Your eyes are the window,
Your eyes are the window to your Soul.

The Window to Your Soul

Religious Connections

The church bell strikes seven. In the morning. The summer of 2018. I am in a shepherds' hut in a field at the foot of the South Downs in the village of Firle in Sussex. Adjacent to the church. There is a slight chill in the air, so I slide back under the duvet but sneak my arm out to turn on the radio to action my early morning habit of the *Today* programme. Shortly, I will complete the first ritual of my day. I will light the tiny, but very effective stove to warm things up, before lighting the gas ring to heat the kettle for a morning brew. When I have woken up properly, I will lie in bed doing my alternate nostril breathing exercises and a meditation. And plan and possibly start the purpose of my short stay here, which is to write. Chiefly about what feels like the fitting choice given my current location – my religious connections. If I am lucky I will spend time with the vicar. Talk with him about his own life and experiences. To hear from him in person having read several of his books that have been both inspiring and entertaining.

I love a good church. To sit in. To reflect in. To be peaceful in. To pray in, in my own way. For quiet contemplation. As a place of sanctuary, peace and tranquillity. Sacred as places of worship but which conjure up feelings of curiosity, and magnificent because of sheer architectural splendour or simplicity. I was brought up beside a church and always feel comforted by the sound of church bells. To be precise, we were brought up in a square with a church at its centre. But I confess that the tennis club at one corner and my cousins' homes on all sides stole more of my time and interest when I was young.

A good churchyard is also something I find hard to resist. They fill me with wonder about the people held there, their histories and heritage.

In August 2017, Marg and I found ourselves in a churchyard in the heart of Wales, which was even more tranquil and beautiful than usual because of its personal connections. We were unexpectedly meandering along the wonderful mid-Welsh roads on our way up to north Wales, when we realised we were passing through the tiny hamlet of Pennant Melangell. Suddenly the turning was upon us. "We just have to, don't we?", I asked and before Marg could answer, I swept the car into the tiny, winding track that takes you down the valley to the church. Slowly we passed streams, sheep-filled fields, wild flowers, overhanging trees and rickety bridges, at the edge of which were wide open and untamed lands supported by the rising hills and mountains of the Tanat valley. The side of the track was teeming with pheasants and partridges. It had been 4 or 5 years since our last visit and since we were so close, we thought we would probably just pop in, take another look around and be on our way.

It was a Sunday and as we approached the heavy, wooden side doors, we realised there was a service in progress. We paused outside the door and were soon joined by a few other curious souls who had taken the time to go out of their way to pay their respects to this unique place. We all hovered. This wasn't the sort of church to be so packed with worshippers that you could just sidle in and join the throng anonymously. To go in would have meant a noteworthy interruption. After a few minutes, and it felt in keeping with this most contemplative of places, a most thoughtful gentleman opened the door to us and ushered us quietly and calmly in to a pew.

We sat happily through the remainder of the short service by which time we had agreed via hastily scribbled notes to each other that we would stay. We wanted to see if we could engage with any of the small congregation or staff to see what information they may be able to offer us, and perhaps we could offer them in return, about my maternal great-grandfather. He was the rector there at St Melangell's church. And it was from this most stunning of valleys in the heart of Powys that he ministered to his flock from 1893.

After the service, we both started talking to different people and it soon materialised that not only did I have some history to share with them, but they had a revelation for me. We were taken up into the loft. It held a small museum and we were shown a book that identified exactly when my great-grandfather had been the rector there. And, employing my own powers of deduction and through excited conversation, as more people got involved, it was revealed that he may well have been buried in the churchyard outside.

We knew that my grandmother had been orphaned at a young age, so it was apparent that if her father had been the rector from 1893, the chances were that he either died whilst still the rector or may at least have still been living in the area. Therefore, it was likely he had been laid to rest at St Melangell. Someone then revealed that there was a book containing the names of everyone in the graveyard. Sure enough, on scouting through not only did we see his name but there, in the same grave was his wife, my great-grandmother.

Our little gaggle bustled out of the church and quickly found the plot, in all its faded glory. The gravestone of my great-grandparents. I looked down upon it proudly. Although so distant in that moment, I felt very close to them. I had photographs and stories of them, but the poignancy of this moment stirred a real bond in me. I committed there and then to return that way a week later equipped with cleaning tools to smarten up their resting place. Which I did.

But what else about religion holds my fascination? Am I religious? What does it even mean to be religious? I am not religious in any conventional sense. I don't go to church or follow a particular faith and its principles. I don't know if I believe in a God or gods or Jesus Christ. I still question those things. I find it hard to dismiss the teachings of different religions out of hand and wouldn't be so disrespectful as to dismiss so many wise and educated people who do follow a religion. Nor would I take a cynical view, believing that they have been deceived in some way. Religion could be seen as a form of magic in that it doesn't exist but we allow ourselves to be taken along by it. It takes people into a different world. Perhaps of make believe. Perhaps a false sense of security. I surmise. I do believe in the principles associated with many religions, those meant to alleviate oppression and as a fight against injustice. But I regard those as general principles of humanity rather than necessarily to be defined as "religious". Sometimes I have actually wondered whether in fact it would have been good for me to have been religious. Perhaps it is satisfying and comforting to have a deep and genuine faith.

Many people prefer to identify as spiritual rather than religious. I have chosen in recent years, inspired by and encouraged because of poor health, to meditate. I certainly find this helpful. Allowing for contemplation, reflection, clarity. It is a very commonplace practice for

My family had grown up with my maternal grandparents and so had been fairly well versed in my grandmother's background. But as with most people's histories, when you delve a little deeper more rises to the surface. Nain (Welsh for grandmother) lost both of her parents before she was 10, but had retained some contact, with one of her brothers, and in later years a second brother. (Little is known of a third brother.)

My grandmother was well educated, firstly at Howells School in Denbigh and afterwards at Cambridge University, where in 1915 (3 years before women won the vote and 32 years before degrees were awarded to women at Cambridge) she gained a Mathematics Tripos from Girton College. Her education during her school years, we understand, being paid for by the clergy.

St Melangell was said to be, "An Irish girl whose father arranged for her to marry a chieftain back in AD 607– but she would have none of it, and joined the great band of Irish hermits who came across the sea, and founding small stone cells in lovely valleys, preached the Christian Gospel to the pagan Celts. The maiden's name was Monacella in Latin. Melangell became her Welsh name. She found her way to the Pennant Valley in the 7th century, and the legend tells of her praying on a stone slab outside her hut one day when Prince Brochwel – one of the princes of Powys – came hunting hares in the valley. A hare ran under Melangell's skirt for protection. The huntsman's horn stuck to his lips. The hounds backed away in fear. The prince was so impressed by the maiden's godliness that he gave her the valley, as a sanctuary for man and beast. The hares were called Melangells Lambs and were protected. Still today if you see one of these beautiful, shy creatures, you shout God and Melangell be with you."

Melangell built a wooden church, which was replaced in the 12th century with a stone building. Within this Norman Church is the shrine to St Melangell, and her bones lie inside the reliquary. The shrine dates from AD 1160 and is the earliest surviving Romanesque shrine in northern Europe.

I have a slightly surreal sense that there were some similarities between St Melangell and her namesake, my grandmother, not least in regarding them both as part of a very small band of trailblazers for feminism and women. Both pioneers in their way. Determined and strong women!

many people today, perhaps in place of more conventional forms of religious practice, or simply to provide stability and a calming of the mind and body.

I have no opposition to religion other than where it is forced upon people, especially by politicians claiming that their decision-making processes have divine intervention, which I find hard to take. Are they not equipped to make decisions without? I also object where it is misconstrued or used in such an obsessive way that it causes hatred and harm. Acts carried out in the name of different religions, and horrors of old that have come to light in recent years, are frightening. These cases are shocking. They also lead to categorisation and can breed intolerance. They distance people because of stigmas associated with them and the genuine, honest fact of just being religious or belonging to a certain religion. But I don't believe that being religious necessarily means oppression and lack of reason. I do see that as a generalisation in the same way that stating that the acts of one oppressor define their religion as a whole. People can be very quick to identify themselves and other people which seems to be a characteristic of the age we live in and often many of us do that by claiming that we are not religious. Why is that? Why do we have to identify as anything?

I read somewhere a few months ago, that Pope Francis had purportedly said, "It is not necessary to believe in God to be a good person. In a way, the traditional notion of God is outdated. One can be spiritual but not religious. It is not necessary to go to church and give money. For many, nature can be a church. Some of the best people in history did not believe in God, while some of the worst deeds were done in His name." I found this surprising and my doubt in him saying those things was confirmed but whoever did say them I think put things very appropriately in his name.

"This is my simple religion. There is no need for temples; no need for complicated philosophy. Our own brain, our own heart is our temple; the philosophy is kindness." Dalai Lama. I believe that the Dalai Lama did actually say that and in a simpler way reflects a way of thinking that I think many of us would run with.

I didn't have religion pushed upon me when I was young. In fact, as a very small child my mother removed us (not forcibly) from Sunday school at St Paul's, which sat at the heart of the square where we lived. She felt that it had become too "high church" and rather too evangelical but nevertheless it stood as a significant and monumental structure in the first 18 years of my life. I wasn't encouraged towards religion. I wasn't discouraged. It wasn't a topic of conversation or interest in my family. I can only suppose that to have been a good thing as it enabled each of us, if we chose, to make our own minds up and our own choices.

None of my immediate family were religious as far as I am aware. Nor was anyone what would now be referred to as spiritual. That would possibly have been looked down upon, and indeed some members of our broader family were positively agnostic. But when it came to O level and A level choices for myself, religious knowledge was on my hit list.

What drew me to this choice for someone with no apparent or obvious faith, religious convictions or background? It may have been more a process of elimination that was not uncommon then, career requirements not being given the due consideration that they tend to be given today. I leant heavily towards the arts and humanities. I wasn't a scientist and certainly missed out on the immense gift of the mathematics gene of my maternal grandmother, despite her extra efforts in helping with my homework. Neither was I a linguist. Teachers can be hugely influential, not necessarily with their powers of persuasion, but by their devotion to their subject, and in how inspiring they may be, and I do recall my Religious Education (R.E.) teacher bringing that subject to life for me, opening up an understanding of the wider world, its differences and the degrees of tolerance required to appreciate those and remain open minded. R.E. wasn't just about bible studies. It was about world religions, history, philosophy and so much more. Those things captured my imagination and to a degree have remained with me.

For perhaps similar reasons I went on to study R.E. (with sports studies) at college as part of a joint humanities honours degree. That was certainly more by necessity than design, following on from the debacle of my A levels and having to scramble a second A level in addition to English, in my retakes.

Moving on to other connections. A song on the album that accompanies this book, "Strange People", came about because of a religious inspiration. When visiting Cadiz in early 2018, I took myself to the Roman amphitheatre. They have created wonderful depictions allowing you to imagine what it would have been like back in those days when performances were put on there. I was fascinated by the references to areas of the theatre being set aside for different strata of society. I imagined it as a theatre of dreams. And within that I started to explore the links between religion and theatre. Religious practices and dramatic presentation share many common elements: costume, storytelling, a place to play and an audience. Also, many of the world's dramatic forms are derived from religious rituals and are still, in some way, connected to religious celebration. Drama, it could be said, has had a long sometimes intimate, sometimes adversarial relationship with religion. I would ask forgiveness of some of you at this point by also requesting that football be included to make up a trio here. Cult followings, the fervour, the passion invoked. There is an almost religious following amongst many football teams and their fans and Old Trafford, the home of Manchester United, is known as the theatre of dreams.

And so, it is time to leave having spent a few days again in this wonderful place. I have written. I have reflected. I don't know if I have come up with any answers about the bond that I feel I have with religion, faith, spirituality. I didn't get to have afternoon tea with the vicar. I didn't even see him this time. Any questions I have will have to wait a while. A bond is an interesting thing. In the same way that I feel that I have a bond with religion, faith, spirituality for several reasons I had almost felt drawn to this place when I first came here a few years ago and to the stories and background relating to it that I have read so much about. To things that I can't put my finger on. To the place and to the man who ministers here and qualities in both that I find intriguing. I will return of that I am sure. "Put the kettle on Reverend, I'm coming back."

Strange people,
Buzzing round' like birds.
Strange people
Not writing to be heard.

Religious Conversations

In exploring all of these connections, my own beliefs and religious heritage, I opened up a conversation with Marg about religion – her background and relationship with it being very different from my own. This is a snapshot of that conversation.

M: So Marg on religion for 10 minutes.

J: Yes, you're limited.

M: I grew up in a household where Sunday was the Sabbath. That was part of Northern Irish culture and particularly Protestant culture. We were Presbyterian, which is of course a wee bit better than being Protestant; we were a wee bit better than the ordinary Protestants. What it meant was that as a country there were no shops open, no cinema open, the swimming pools weren't open on a Sunday. You weren't supposed to go and play on the swings, you weren't allowed to watch TV. The only thing you were really allowed to do was read a book or play board games. But other than that, Sunday was the day of rest. Especially when I was younger, it was quite a Calvinist approach to Sunday. What it meant then also was that we would all have to go to church. That was the ritual, so we'd all get up and mum and dad would have to get us all dressed, all five of us kids out of the house in our Sunday best dress – whatever it was – and we'd all have to go to church. One of them, either my mum or my dad or my Aunty who lived with us, would stay at home to cook lunch. All the rest of us would troop off to church. It was always very stressful and we were always the late family so we would have to come in, into our little pew, through the side door. Hopefully we'd make it there before 11.30am when I think the service was. The kids, after about half an hour, would troop out to Sunday school and the adults would stay. We would've had Sunday school in the middle of the church service. It was a complete ritual and it was non-negotiable; there was no question of people not going, it was just absolutely what had to happen. Church was one of those things that was a bit like school where you can be a bit naughty. Dad occasionally – whenever the minister started doing the sermon – would produce some sweets and pass them along the pew and so we'd all have a little sweetie. We'd try not to rustle the wrappers and that was the height of scandal or subterfuge, really, to this puritanical Sabbath upbringing.

J: How old were you throughout this?

M: This was primary school up until 11 or 12, something like that. I'll come to that later. It was up until I left home at 16, actually. It was every week. Sometimes we were so horribly late - if we were more than 5 minutes late, my parents were horribly embarrassed. The other church was called Ballygrainey and this started at 12 o'clock. It was a country church just outside of the town. It was really tiny, so when all of us trooped in as seven people, we doubled the congregation. We hated Ballygrainey because you were really exposed and so you couldn't fiddle or rustle. The great story in the family was: we all went into Ballygrainey and it was Palm Sunday and the minister started preaching and he was talking about the importance of Palm Sunday and that Jesus was on the road to the crucifixion and he rode to Jerusalem sitting on his ass, at which point the whole of the room started to snigger and shake. You weren't allowed to laugh at Ballygrainey because everybody could see, so that wasn't good. So that's what the upbringing was. I certainly didn't enjoy religion. It was something that was a bit like school, something you had to put up with. I think what happened is that, when I was about 11 or 12 and became more self-aware, I began to see it as something that was really institutional as opposed to something that was personal. In Northern Ireland, of course, it was institutional. In fact, it's completely tribal. Some people have personal religion and that's fine; I'm quite tolerant of people who are personally religious. But I'm quite intolerant of people who are tribally religious. I find that really unappealing because it smacks of intolerance and self-righteousness, which is what I really rail against. Northern Ireland for me really smacked of suffocation and the requirement to conform. If you didn't conform, it was quite dangerous and I do mean quite literally dangerous. Your life would be at risk. For us, for example, it was really important what religion your boyfriend was. It was really important you didn't get into a mixed marriage. People of mixed marriages would get bricks through their window. You were personally, physically at risk of violence if you were part of a mixed marriage. So that's how tribal it got. Why should anyone throw a brick through a window just because of what religion you were? It wasn't what you believed but it was what you were born into; you had no choice as to whether you were Catholic or Protestant. That whole institutionalising of religion I find really, really just so repugnant. It's a bit like people who are born - are you born a Muslim? You might be born into a Muslim culture but what does that say about your personal religion? Let's not just stereotype people, let's allow people to have their personal beliefs. It's quite distinctive from wrapping everybody up in a wrapper that says because you were born into that family therefore you must be Protestant or Muslim or whatever.

J: Can I just ask you a question because you haven't read my updated draft on the subject of religious connections and so on. I talk about a lot of things that you've referred to, like intolerance and tolerance, and the whole thing about having things pushed on you. I'm introducing you into this picture because I didn't have religion pushed upon me and that's why in some ways I'm so interested in why I have an interest in religion and things that are spiritual. I clearly have some interest from when I was young and that's why I studied world religions (RE) and so on. You've used the word tribal quite often and what I've done in my very early draft for this section is to liken religion to theatre and to football. Certainly within football there is a tribal element because there's that fervour, passion, that cult following almost really. I just wanted to pick up on that, actually.

M: Absolutely. With football and religion they go completely hand-in-hand and it's tribal. With Northern Ireland it's like Scotland with Celtic and Rangers. I'm trying to think of the teams in Ireland… it's Glentoran.

J: Georgie Best, my hero, started off playing with Glentoran.

M: I can't remember the Catholic team.

J: Like Rangers and Celtic.

M: It's very similar. If you're born into a Celtic family you can't support Rangers can you, because that would just be abhorrent and you would lose friends. You lose friends over religion in Northern Ireland. I'm just more of a free spirit. I respect personal belief but I almost disrespect people who believe it because it's the way it's always been and because it's institutional. I find that very oppressive.

J: I agree with you and that's kind of where I've been going when I've asked myself for this book whether I'm actually religious or spiritual, what my actual beliefs are and what my thinking is, which is quite different from just being interested and having a curiosity.

M: What's interesting now is that, I think as a result of that, I escaped from the institutional religious obligations when I "ran away", when I left Northern Ireland. I would always - much to my parents' upset, really - when I went home, not go to church with them because going to church was this weird quasi-social occasion where you'd get shown off. I couldn't even go to church with them. I couldn't combine any respect for their personal beliefs with this kind of social ritual of being seen to turn up to church and stuff. So, I didn't go to church when I went home once I'd left home. That's when I didn't do it and they really tried to get me to go and I wouldn't so there was a lot of pressure on me during my 20s and then they sort of gave up. On a personal level, I even found carol services really difficult. I remember I went to a carol service with you once at Clapham Common and just having tears. The weird thing is…

J: I hasten to add that we were in our 30s by then.

M: …when you're brought up in a very profound institutional ritual and then you reject it, when you're pulled back into that – and if you don't like it – the strength of that, the dichotomy, the pull and the push of that is really powerful and I just had tears. It seemed silly because it was just a bloody carol service. You're only going there and singing a few songs. There's no pressure at all.

J: It was the association.

M: Yeah, exactly. I'm over that now but I did find that really difficult. What's nice is that I now feel I can handle religion when it's personal; If somebody comes to me and says, "I'm a Buddhist," I certainly believe and tolerate what people believe. I think what's interesting is when it comes to the social bit, like the carol service or that sort of thing, I can now handle it. When I went back for mum's and dad's funerals, (and it's interesting because it's all learned behaviour) is that I knew exactly what we were going to do and when we were going to do it and how it was going to work. It was like second nature. It was like a Pavlovian reaction about what to do at the funeral service and how to behave and all of that kind of stuff. It was just completely second nature. So, in a funny way that was weird because it was really familiar but it was also something I'd rejected.

J: Do you know what that's also made me think about? You can come back to that because it's very personal but if I don't say this now I may well forget what it is I'm trying to say: I have this issue with funerals, which is that I don't believe that you have to go to funerals. There are a couple of points I want to make here. One is that not going to somebody's funeral a few years ago got me into deep poo poo with a very good friend. That wasn't because I don't believe that you have to go to funerals.

I actually wholeheartedly committed to going to this person's father's funeral. I was very simply unwell. I think perhaps I hadn't emphasised that at that time. Sometimes I had to bail out of things and that was just the way I had to exist. I'm very sorry that that happened. The other thing is that because of the way I grew up, and was brought up, perhaps I have a different take on the importance of attending a religious experience in a church when somebody dies. I think I remember there were times when I was growing up when there were members of the family who died and another member of that family didn't go to the funeral and I certainly don't remember that person being ostracised or anything. That was somebody's choice, really. Somebody recently mentioned to me they knew somebody they were reasonably close to had died and said, "I guess I'll have to go to the funeral." I said, "Well, you don't have to." I don't think people should feel they have to go to a funeral as a matter of duty or obligation. You can show your respect in other ways actually. It's terribly conventional going to a funeral. It's very, very conventional and your love and respect for people can be shown in other ways and for the people close to the people who have died.

M: I would agree with that completely. It's very consistent with me saying I'm intolerant of religion for social reasons and the institution of it, really. I was just reflecting for me. I wanted to be at my parents' funeral and it was a lovely, lovely family time and for me that was a lovely, lovely time. But when I think about how that relates to religion, how completely instinctive my knowledge and behaviour was. That ritual had been so embedded in me. Even now, I can sing the hymns and sing my choruses.

J: You certainly know them better than me!

M: That's quite interesting. What it leaves me with is a sort of lingering - where I am now - a lingering feeling. I think the lingering feeling is between knowing and respecting other people's religious beliefs and having some level of spirituality myself. I don't believe that there was a man called Jesus who died on the cross and we are all going to get raised into heaven and everlasting life. I don't believe in any of that in any literal sense. I'd like to think I kind of appreciate a bit of reflection and meditation and being a better person and the best you can be, that kind of spirituality in a secular sense. There's a sort of dilemma there. That's what a lot of funerals are about or that's what a lot of Christmas is about or even other celebrations - they are about having a moment to reflect. The flip side of that is thinking, "This is

24

a load of trite. This is a load of codswallop," and it's sentimental and there to make you feel, "lalalala and we'll go out and get pissed". The triteness of it. It's just there for showing off for the institutional reasons and saying that you turned up. It's interesting that whole thing and the extent to which ritual is important for society and community and the extent to which I appreciate it as long as it has integrity.

J: I think integrity is a really important word.

M: I reject it when it just remains only a social norm and kind of then lacks integrity. I think that then gives two fingers up to the social norms. I'm stuck in a kind of pro-con about it, I suppose.

J: While you're pausing, something that came up on social media the other day and I think it was quite interesting. It was quoting a lot of political leaders who claim that God intervened as part of their decision-making processes and some of those people I respect hugely and admire – others maybe I don't. I think I have commented on that in this section in the book. I was interested to know what your take might be on that.

M: Complete bollocks. That's just moving to the world of self-righteous, "I am right because God tells me so," Well I'm sorry, no. What you can say is, "My job is to make a decision if we're going to go to war or something and this is the best decision I can make. That's honest. It might be wrong, it might be right but that's the best I can do and that's my job and that's the position I've got,"

J: I think your take on that is clear and that's exactly what I said. In a way it's a real shame. The question I asked when somebody put that on social media at the time was, "Why do they have to do that? Why do they have to introduce God into their decision-making process or suggest that they have done?" And the question is, "Why can't they make decisions on their own anyway?". They've supposedly been voted into office to do that and their responsibility surely is to be capable of making a decision with their advisers around them and I use "advisers" quite often in inverted commas. I think that that's wholly intolerable, actually. That's just a typical example of what you've been talking about.

M: … If they put it in a different … it's also about language and generation.

J: I'm talking about people in our generation.

———

M: My parents might say that. They might say, "I really don't know what to do," if it's a really difficult decision. They might say, "Well I just prayed." If they didn't know what to do about a particular problem or whatever.

J: That's fine – to a degree.

M: That's their softer version of saying "I asked God". What somebody nowadays might say is, "Well, I meditated on it," or "I just decided to go away for 2 days and had a long weekend to really reflect." So the fact that some people then say "I asked God and God told me …" that becomes much too …

J: That's what I'm referring to.

M: … That's back to the whole thing of them grabbing God and institutionalising it and saying, "This being has told me," instead of taking personal responsibility for it. I have one more thing to say about all of this, which is that one of the things that annoys me so much is the whole infallibility of the Pope and the Catholic church and all that thing. It epitomises an institutional religion. This whole anti-abortion, anti-contraception – still anti-contraception in this world?! What is the Pope bloody thinking of? This is bonkers! And not only bonkers, the fact that the Pope is the God on Earth. And then the Vatican is so bloody corrupt. So that's got a complete lack of integrity and institution and paedophilia in the church in Ireland. That's why this institutional stuff gets me – you can see – it makes me really angry and that's what I reject.

J: Agreed. Thank you.

Travel

Island Life

Once I was into my teens, my holidays were spent mainly with my mum who relied, at this time, on the kindness of friends to host us at their home on the Isle of Wight. We spent several weeks there one summer, not in their house but in a very ramshackle caravan in a beautifully leafy glade in Whitton. Mum, my middle sister, myself and at various other times either my sister's boyfriend or a school friend of mine. It was a fun time. Crammed into the van at night, I did my darnedest to send everyone to sleep happy with my best Hilda Baker and Frank Goodwin impersonations. On one occasion my sister, my friend and I got dolled up in long dresses and were taken by Mum to a disco. More of a nightclub really. The other two got friendly with two French sailors. I met a very charming German boy and arranged to meet him on Ryde pier the following day. Sadly, that assignation was forbidden, Mum citing the fact that we could not trust the Germans. "He could be a spy," she stated from the driver's seat. This was not said in jest and I balked not only at the frustration of being held captive but by how ridiculous it was. I find it hard to believe that she actually thought that and said it, but I remember it. Perhaps it was the first thing she could think of when I protested.

When holidays were still taken as a family, we went one time to Malta. One evening we went to what can only be described as a swanky cabaret style restaurant, to eat and be entertained by a well known, but now disgraced, Australian entertainer. He took a shine to one of my sisters and picked her out of the audience to, "sing up". Being the focus of attention and joining in with group activities were not popular pastimes for her. We came away proudly with signed, personally drawn cartoons. It is curious today to recall events such as this and how times have changed for many of the people involved. Why did he select my 13-year-old sister to, "sing up"? There certainly wasn't anything threatening about that evening but as we have discovered, some things were not as innocent as they appeared to be in those days. Was is that people turned a blind eye or were frightened of the consequences of speaking out, or actually thought such behaviour acceptable? I believe that it was a combination of those things.

In these days of #MeToo, I will share a story from another of our Isle of Wight holidays that highlights how we are prepared sometimes to keep quiet about situations that maybe we should not. During one long summer when staying at our friends' house, just outside a sleepy village on the south side of the island, I would sometimes take walks on my own. A bored 16-year-old looking for something to do. One evening, I took off at dusk and ambled down the hill, hands in jean pockets, quite possibly kicking a pebble or two as I went. In the village, I passed a small cluster of local lads doing what local lads do in small villages. Leaning on their bikes. Some smoking. Chewing gum. Chewing the fat. I'm not sure what I thought I'd find down there. There was, and is, a pub, but I was too young to go there. I just needed to get out of the house, let off steam, burn up some youthful adrenaline. Having satisfied myself that there wasn't much of interest to me, I turned and started wandering back up the hill to join my family back at the house. One of the boys took it upon himself to accompany me, walking alongside with his bike. A muscular, earthy teenager with fair hair, sallow skin and a hint of stubble, dressed in check shirt, faded jeans and desert boots befitting the style of the time. A hint of musk and testosterone. I don't remember if we talked or not. Was I finding the situation exciting, some adventure that I had been seeking? By this time, it was dark. No street lights. Nothing of note in terms of houses. The only sound was that of cows settling down for the night. I don't remember what led up to it but at the top of the hill before turning into the track, I found myself roadside, lying on the verge with the boy lying beside me or was he on top of me? There was some kissing and fumbling and I confess that I don't recall either whether I felt that he was forcing himself upon me or whether I was agreeable to the situation, at least initially. I'm not sure if I felt fear. Maybe a little, because I do remember saying, "I could just shout and my family will hear me." I suspect from that very vivid memory that I had started to become concerned about where this was leading. Was I encouraging him or just humouring him, thinking he would just decide to bid me a polite good night and be off? Either way, the bit of rough and tumble ended, possibly when he realised that I wasn't a pushover. Perhaps because he thought I would be heard shouting for help, or perhaps because he was actually a decent, sensible bloke. He took off on his bike and I trotted down to the house my adrenaline rush more than I'd bargained for. Conversation barely stopped when I appeared. The TV didn't either. I was back. Life had carried on as normal inside but outside, for a short while on that summer's night, for me it hadn't. I have never spoken of this. Rightly or wrongly, I never considered it important enough. I hope that he was a decent bloke and that my not saying anything didn't give him a blueprint for how he should go on behaving.

If adventure was what I had been looking for on holiday, then a year later I was to find it in no uncertain terms. When I would start to understand the meaning of freedom, its benefits, when you have it, and some of the downfalls, when you don't.

Travel

To Russia with Love

At the tender age of 17, in June of the baking hot summer of 1976, having successfully passed my driving test and sensing the welcome proximity of adulthood, I embarked on what will always remain one of the trips of my lifetime. I went to Russia.

This was an opportunity that had come up at school. As the time drew near for departure and indeed by the time the day arrived, I knew that I would be surrounded by not one person that I knew or even from my hometown. I would be away from home and anything familiar for the first time, without any family or friends, for the best part of a month. No mobiles in those days and in reality, given where we would be, little or no means of communication at all. But I was not alone. I would be sharing this Eastern bloc excursion with more than thirty other 17–19 year olds, two experienced drivers, our leader and his second in command. We were a bunch of intrepid, brave or crazy, adventure seekers thrown together and ready to have our eyes and minds opened – although in those first few days, and when planning to go on the trip, we naively had no idea quite to what extent this would happen.

I have no recollection about how supportive my parents were nor whether I met with any opposition, but they seemed to be behind this wish and for that I was grateful. I do remember, when also wanting to do a Camp America type trip before sixth form, that it was a firm no. In the run up to Russia, I was living again with my mum in our old family home. My life was quite calm after a turbulent few years living with my dad and I was full of dreams and character-building notions. With Russia, I thought I was onto a winner and that my life would soar into the happy unknown from there on in. I imagine that events of recent years for both of my parents had left them content to let things be. They possibly deemed it kinder on themselves and me to let me go, although I would have thought that an American summer camp was a safer bet for their youngest daughter than journeying behind the Iron Curtain. Perhaps I got this wrong and they saw it as a real-life experience. If they were so measured in their analysis, then they got that spot on.

So, the group assembled somewhere in the Midlands, drove to Harwich and then a ferry across to Ostend where we got our first experience of what would be a food staple for the next few weeks, served from a hatch in the back of the coach, namely tinned meat and sandwich spread. Those two things have stayed with me. A little like that alcoholic beverage that you get terribly drunk on that first time and which will never be forgotten nor consumed again.

And then we set sail in our hot, sweaty and excited sardine can across Belgium, Germany, Austria, Hungary, Romania to Russia. Leaving the coach in Odessa and flying to Moscow on a very small Aeroflot machine, being served boiled sweets en route. Returning to Kiev to our trusty truck and homeward via Czechoslovakia and back through Germany and Belgium.

Most of the geopolitical landscape has changed now and certain towns and cities belong to different countries. Socially, politically and economically many things are different now too.

The focus of this trip was going to be on communist Eastern Europe, one-party states, where freedom did not exist for the majority of the population. Transportation, communication and economic fluidity has moved on a great deal since then. Those things did not exist in the same way in the countries we were venturing into then, they were more often than not non-existent and with punishment for transgressions a serious business.

We were almost completely ignorant about the reality for people living in those countries. We had been advised to take plenty of Wrigley's chewing gum, maybe some spare blue jeans and other items not easily attainable to the people there, but with which we could show our appreciation for the welcome shown to us. At times, we did feel like animals in a zoo as we made our way down hillsides and through quiet villages. The children, dressed in no more than rags, would somehow be able to pre-empt the very rare Western coaches passing through and come rushing up with outstretched hands as we threw things out of the window to them. We were a complete novelty to these eager, smiling faces.

We had raced along, stopping memorably in Frankfurt for one evening where a small group of us encountered continental café society for the first time. We enjoyed outdoor tables along narrow cobbled streets, the trusting nature of serving food and drink before taking payment, unattended by adults, eating a tasty pizza and drinking a beer. Then, thrilled by the challenge, we did a successful dine and dash. You have to do it once in your lifetime and if you can't when you're 17 then I'm not sure when is appropriate. I accept no responsibility for any person under the age of 21 doing this having read this book, but would heartily encourage you to do it at least once before you are 30.

My memories from this trip are a myriad of jumbled up things. Referring to a photograph album I still have, I have been able to piece together our route but where and at what stage of the trip some things happened are less certain.

Our accommodation along the way was always rough. Generally small shacks or chalets, in Moscow university halls – stark even compared to the ones I was to know as a student and sometimes they were extremely bleak. Bed bugs abounded. Thin, damp mattresses were the norm. I don't remember any bathrooms, but stopping off to go to a loo as we drove through a town in Romania we had to use a barn, squatting on the floor along with everyone else, straw replacing loo paper and any sewage system.

We visited many very special places: Vienna which I have been fortunate enough to revisit in rather more stylish circumstances, even enjoying a private performance by the famous Vienna Boys Choir; Karlsruhe, Budapest where we gazed wide eyed at the beauty of the Danube and watched players playing on their giant chess board on a hillside, overlooking the river. Sleepy Romanian villages and small towns. Swimming in the Black Sea in Odessa where I am ashamed to say I fell asleep during a performance of La Traviata in the Odessa Opera and Ballet theatre. My James Bond moment on the Hungarian/Romanian border where our coach was searched and the drivers quietly went around our group, checking that we were not carrying any currency from the country we were leaving. I was. We surreptitiously ventured round to the coach boot, extracted my case and the money contained in it and slipped it into a bin without any qualms. The border guards were pleasant enough when looking through my belongings and seemed to enjoy asking after everyone in my pocket photograph album. Perhaps there was something shady in the looks of my family. We played frisbee in the Carpathian Mountains and swam in the lakes there. And continued to eat sandwich spread. Prague, on our return journey, seemed like a world away from what we had been used to for the previous few weeks, which felt like months. It was westernised, at least by the standards of the other countries we had been in. We ate hamburgers, wandered freely, and in the quiet and calm of a bedroom, the drivers revealed to three of our party the truths of what had been going on in our time in Russia. Apart from making some great mates on this trip, I got very close to one or two of the boys. It felt like a lifetime although in reality any relationships were fleeting and transient. We sought comfort, support and company with each other, quite innocent in our little world, which was a real protective blanket against the goings on around us.

Hungary and Romania had been tough. We had seen a lot of poverty, the likes of which these days you would only experience in third world countries. But unlike some of those places and my knowledge of the ones I have visited since, or that people close to me have witnessed where the people and the landscapes can still seem hopeful, there was a bleakness about these countries at that time for me. Russia was another ball game again. We witnessed so much that I hope I will be forgiven if have got things mixed up. One night somewhere in Russia, possibly Odessa, we all assembled for a party on the grass near to our chalets. Someone had acquired vodka and it was flowing freely and we were happy, high-spirited, but well behaved. And then the jeeps rolled in, the soldiers jumped out – machine guns in hand, and that was the end of our fun for that night. Except it wasn't. The condition of some of our chalets was so dire that some of us decamped to the coach to sleep. Some German people were staying in the chalets on the edge of the car park and in the middle of the night the jeeps rolled up again but this time they beat on the chalet doors, dragged some people out, attacked them and left.

We saw all the sights in Moscow. We queued for 4 hours to see the supposed body of Lenin. Red Square, the Gum Store, boys with machine guns guarding monuments. Peroxide beehives, powder-blue crimplene coats. Locals queuing for hours to buy small quantities of rationed food. Some of the braver (or more foolish) amongst our party exchanged their jeans for Red Army belts which they managed somehow to wear under their underpants all the way home without detection.

What didn't go undetected, given that we had an Intourist courier accompanying us for the whole 3 days in Moscow, was the strength with which our leader disliked the communist system. He spoke quite openly about his feelings and opinions. Intourist was the state travel agency responsible for organising the great majority of foreigners travel within the Soviet Union. Rather more than a guide, they ensured that you only travelled where they wanted you to go. And presented the Soviet Union in a favourable light to impressionable teenagers.

The truths that were revealed to some of us in Prague, were that our leader, he of the loose tongue, had been cautioned in Kiev, our next stop after Moscow and where we returned to meet our coach. I do remember him being taken into a hotel on the chalet site. He was warned that he had to stop his anti-communist propaganda, or he would be detained. For the remaining 3 days of our time in Russia as we headed for the Czech border, we had a helicopter following us to ensure he left. I suspect they may also have bugged the coach to guard against any unwanted speech.

This was an extraordinary time. When I finally got home I was so overwhelmed that I found it almost impossible to speak to people for many days, maybe weeks. In a way, you have so many thoughts and feelings inside you that they seem scrambled and need sorting out. Naturally everyone I came into contact with demanded to know how my trip had been. It was as though I'd hot footed it to Skegness for the weekend. I simply didn't know where to start. I had so much to digest. I had so many things to sort out in my own mind; exactly what I had seen and experienced. I needed time to think about everything and put those thoughts into some order and into the context of my own life. I needed time to return to my life.

I stayed in touch with several of the group for many years and we met up again for a reunion in London in the late summer of 1978. A lot had changed for me by then and I slowly lost touch with most of my fellow travellers as the years progressed. My photographs, souvenirs and memories stay with me.

Home

Hometown

I've come across many pieces written and performed about the subject of home recently. Research into what home means to us. How it can be defined. In relation to migration. In relation to the musical term "coming home" and returning to the home chord. There seems to be a growing trend with regards to exploring what this word means. So, I'm going to join in.

When I wrote the songs for This Girl, This Woman someone commented that there were a lot of references to places in them. I come from a "broken home". I am a nest builder by nature. I am very "house proud". I have always had a fascination with styling, decorating and designing rooms and spaces. There is an aesthetic impact that is important to me when I spend time in a place, but there is an emotional association too. William Morris commented that everything in a home must be, "either beautiful or functional". I agree. The aesthetics and emotional impact of a place and space are both important to me, and to my enjoyment and contentment – as they are for many people. Some people are less affected, more oblivious to their surroundings and less dependent on them for fulfilment and happiness.

As I write this, I am sitting in the type of space that is a favourite in all ways. I am sat sheltering from the impending rain in an outdoor kitchen next to the retro caravan where I can sleep and lounge. It is basic but functional and pleasing on the eye. I can hear tractors in the distance, but closer to me I hear birds going about their business and the buzzing of dangerously near wasps. One up from camping, I am always happy in these environments, as long as I have a few home comforts provided or packed. These would be a portable loo for those night-time moments, dry matches, a cafetière, teapot, corkscrew and hot water bottle. The interior of the van is decorated in 1970s hues of light brown and pale green florals. Not my first choice but if things go well together, I am satisfied. The kitchen area is made from wooden planks, carefully crafted to provide decking under foot and cover overhead so that you feel as if you are outdoors but protected. It is set in a small patch of Cumbrian woodland. Peaceful and calm, it is a sanctuary, shelter and safe harbour.

I love to sleep and exist in such environments. Free from the trappings of everyday life in the 21st century. I love camping. Glamping would be more exact. Wherever I set up camp I will make a home of it, whatever the limitations.

As a child, I loved to build dens. Perhaps it was about seeking adventure, the opportunity to create, the sense of a den usually being small but always cosy and comforting. Somewhere to hide? My own stab at building a home for myself?

On one occasion, two of my cousins and I built a two-storey den at the edge of a bowling green. It was a magnificent structure. Until we had to abandon it. I had popped around the back of the groundsman's shed to relieve myself only to return and find my two accomplices scarpering and a large, bulbous faced man staring down at my 4'0" self and demanding, "Do you know that you are trespassing?!" "But my Grandfather is a member," I stammered, for want of anything better to say as I took flight.

Why is "home", the sense and significance of it, so important to us? What does it mean? Is it a place – a town or a building – or is it an association? Is it where our roots are originally or where we choose to put them down?

We all come from a home, whatever form it may have taken and wherever it was. It may be one that we remember or not. It may be somewhere we remember fondly or not. It may be somewhere we prefer to forget. Or one we would like to re-create and emulate. They may be homes we moved on to or were forced to leave behind.

The home I grew up in was one I loved very much. No. 6, St Paul's Square, Burton upon Trent (No.6). My maternal great-grandfather had come over from Ireland and built it. My maternal grandfather and my mother had been brought up in it before us. My maternal grandparents continued to live there even when we had moved in. It was big enough to slice it in two, horizontally, allowing for two very well proportioned, four-bedroom, Parisian-style apartments. My grandfather practised medicine in his "rooms" at the back of the house. Dark and really quite gloomy, smoke-stained cream and brown walls, dark wooden furniture, poor lighting, the walls adorned, however, with beautifully painted watercolours of 1920s flapper girls, which we have on our staircase walls now.

This was a home where I built dens out of walk-in broom cupboards. Where an uncle took his own life in our garage. I only realised this recently, having always thought this had taken place at his own home in the north of England. Where we played marbles in the back yard and golf on the "putting" lawn at the front. Where extended family, who lived nearby, gathered often. Where our bright yellow front door was always open to visitors. Where I had my first pets and buried them in my own little patch of the garden. My first hamster buried by mistake when we didn't realise that they went into hibernation. My second and rather aggressive hamster mysteriously managing to escape from a locked cage, prompting a full search of the house.

This house was the source of endless games. Large enough and with so many rooms that Sardines was heaven sent – a rabbit warren of nooks to hide away in making it a real adventure trying to locate each other. We played quizzes in the power cuts of the 1970s. My grandmother, Nain, held regular bridge games in her lounge. Pristinely cut sandwiches, ice buns and eclairs were served, and if we were well-behaved, we were allowed to indulge. We didn't share the strong gin and "IT"s (Italian vermouth) they also drank. When I think of those today, I marvel at their potency and recall the best silver and china tea service, gin-infused voices, plumes of smoke, blue rinses, concentrated looks over pince-nez and wicked women's laughter.

Nain's kitchen was also a generous source of large chunks of white, floury bread with liberal dollops of unsalted butter. One afternoon, it was the scene of some excitement when a cousin went through to put the kettle on, only to be confronted by a cloth-capped stranger holding a swag bag over his shoulder. He fled, spilling his silver haul as he went.

There is cinematic evidence of me as a small child directing traffic on the road outside in my newly acquired policeman's outfit. When I was 10, I had a more serious experience on the road. I was on my bike and took a corner with my hands in the air instead of on the handlebars. Instead of a smooth arrival onto the drive, I slammed into an iron sign post. My bloodied fingerprints remained there for many years to follow.

I had a large, local family of aunts, uncles and cousins. On one occasion, many of us gathered to clear the cellar of junk that had accumulated over decades. We were going to turn it into a rave cave for my eldest sister and cousin. When this job was done, and the cellar put to good use for teenage social activities, us younger family members would very quietly lift the indoor hatch so that we could spy on the goings on of 15-year-olds. (A few years later it would become my own rave cave for similar activities with my friends, until an evicted guest sent a missile through the French windows above the cellar's outdoor entrance and into my grandmother's lounge. I don't know if this was just a pitiful aim and was intended for the cellar door or whether the intention was more malicious. Either way, the brick landed where my grandmother sat watching television. Fortunately, she had just staggered to the toilet. But the cellar days were over.)

By then, most of the good times at No. 6 were over. A short while before, aged 13, my parents' marriage had ended and I was put in the unenviable position of being asked by my father where I would like to live. He asked me this as he was driving me to school one morning. There I was, sitting in the passenger seat of his robust Rover 2500, surrounded by leather upholstery and polished, wooden trim, with him beside me in a stately fashion in the driver's seat. His eyes were fixed firmly on the road ahead as he asked me this. I asked him who my two sisters were going to live with. He said him. So, I said, I would too. Quite apart from this being an impossible position to place any child in, the reality was that I didn't want to go anywhere.

My memory may be putting both my parents in a bad light here. But at that stage in the process, my mother was going to live in a different house with her new partner. My father had bought a new house for himself and remaining at No. 6 with my elderly, disabled grandmother was not an option. I have never stopped to consider what was going to happen to her, if things hadn't turned out as they eventually did. Would she have gone into a care home or stayed in her quarters and rented the remainder of the house? I wonder now what she made of it all?

Whatever my feelings on or understanding of my parents' separation, although I accepted it as fact, I would ultimately have preferred for them to stay together. This is because it would have ensured the continuation of, what I always look back upon as, a harmonious, warm, fairly carefree, at times colourful, childhood. And the continuation of what I knew to be at the centre of that: our home.

I have recently had conversations about this with friends. Either because they have been going through a breakup themselves and wish to do the best by their children, or because they have elected to leave the children in the family home and switch in and out themselves. My contribution, having pondered on this subject over time, is to tell them to try, if possible, to keep the children in the home they have become familiar with. Not to uproot them. Whatever the circumstances of the parental relationship, it only exacerbates any pain by tearing them away from all that they know to be safe and familiar, their comfort and stability.

I went with my father and two sisters to his new home across the river, to the other side of town. It was indeed new. In every sense. Not the big, solid, rambling, home we had come from.

My father's new home was not a happy one for me. He and I fought. We saw my mother regularly and things were extraordinarily amicable between them. I feel proud of them and will always be thankful for this. But my life with my father didn't go well and after a few years I returned to the family home to live with my mother. (My sisters remained with my father; being older, college life was beckoning them.) Mum hadn't left the old family home in the end. She'd been horribly let down by the man she'd given it all up for. So, I was back. But it was a very different home. I had spent a lot of time there in the intervening years but living there again was different. My grandmother had died. My mother was very poorly off and rented a lot of the house out. We lived meagrely with one portable gas heater, which, with some effort, we moved from room to room as and when it was needed. It was a quiet house now. Cold. No longer filled with laughter and curiosity; instead with two people struggling with their various challenges.

It was where I played out a large part of my very own quite troubled youth. Where I experienced real intimacy for the first time with my boyfriend. It is strange to think of the history of the house, the people who had passed through it, and to think of my grandmother's spare room being used for such a purpose – that act taking place only moments before a voice was heard in the hall, "Anyone at home?" My aunt was dropping in from her home across the square. She didn't find us.

It was where I was, by now, coming to realise the true nature of my sexuality and within a year would go through the pain of unrequited love. It was there I suffered the resultant heartache, self-harm, over indulgences, confusion, dismay, and where I failed to gain the A levels that would have taken me away and delivered me to a new world full of optimism. I decided to retake two A levels, but in the end only completed an extra one. "The art teacher and I didn't see eye to eye," artist Jeremy Deller said of his art classes at school. I experienced the same, but I didn't go on to win the Turner Prize. Art and I parted company there and then. My creativity would have to find other ways to manifest itself.

Weathering the storm, brought a positivity into our lives however. My mother undertook refresher training in physiotherapy. She got a job and that, along with the sale of the family home, enabled her to buy her own house. Together, we moved into a little townhouse not far away. It had bags of potential. I had my very own room at the top of the house and I was given carte blanche to decorate it how I wished. Dark browns and creams decked the walls in my bedroom once I had finished, with suitably matching accessories and a few family heirlooms brought with me from around the corner at No.6..

This was the first time I had physically carried out the decoration of my surroundings. As a child, I had also created my own look in my bedroom, paying particular attention to colour schemes that I liked or felt suited to the space in question. This became the beginning of a lifelong passion for interior design, decoration and architecture.

Unexpectedly, our time in the townhouse was short lived. Mum had become very close to a recently widowed family friend who was destined to become my stepfather. He pretty much moved in with us and together the three of us created fun and a sense of security for each other. It was a difficult year for all of us in different ways, but we rode that time out together. In the summer after my 19th birthday, having finally got the grades I needed, we moved to an idyllic countryside cottage on the outskirts of town. With a converted stable housing a flat for their various visiting offspring, me, my two sisters and his daughters, wonderful gardens and a contented atmosphere, it was an incredibly happy home for my mother and stepfather. Mum was settled in her relationship, work and home. The homes of our pasts were now in the past. This was the place that served as a springboard for me to finally fly the family nest, spread my wings and head off to a very different world. I was off to university. I was off to London town.

The Grange

(A tennis club near to No.6 and where I spent a lot of time as a child and teenager.)

Thwack. The smack of a tennis racquet against a ball. The softly mown grass, the white painted lines, the dust trodden patches. The taut, finely wound net, measuring stick, or racquet head. Struggles around the court, lolloping back and forth. Some with an eye, some with the legs. The Tyrolean style pavilion and yet so very English. Square wooden tables. Directors chairs all round. Tea urns, cups and saucers. Homemade cakes. Whose turn to bake this week? Cucumber sandwiches on white. Egg and cress, fish paste on brown. No granary then. No crusts. All pause for tea. Fifteen all. Time to rest. Six o'clock comes. The drinks are poured. The sun sets. Play continues. Until the dew appears, you give of your best. Time to shower. Time to reflect. Water tumbles slowly, Daddy long legs escape their nests ready for an evening of flying into lamplight. "Mine's a shandy for now. Bag of salt and shake crisps." Fish and chips will come later, a game of pontoon, a test. Match boxes adorn the walls. Vimto, Coke. A Bass beer poured – the best.

Dawn rises. Hedgehogs stuck in the netting. Rollers going back and forth. Water being sprayed. Then the hour comes around again. The first cars arrive. Then by foot. By three o'clock the courts are full. The weekend is underway. "Anyone for tennis?" Uncle Pom Pom with his basket full of booze. Auntie with her fags. Daid (a Welsh word for grandfather) raking his radishes. Another auntie feeling chilly. Some in long trousers, some in frilly knickers. All whites without question. Etiquette unspoken. Green Flash. Slazenger, Maxply Dunlop. What's the tension of your gut? The key's behind the tap if you get there early. Games of football on Friday nights. Junior Night, all the talent lined up. Obedient rows. Keen. Racquets to attention.

London Town

"So, essentially you are homeless?"

The year was 1995 and I was visiting my new GP to register. I was living in Brixton, having moved there to be nearer to my girlfriend of a few months, Marg. I had fled South Norwood, my home of 5 years, after a traumatic break-up.

Arriving in Brixton, where I would remain for 10 years, the GP's words whilst blunt, confronted me with my reality. She was right to a certain extent. I have never regarded myself as homeless though. I feel that that would be doing a disservice to people who live on the streets or seek refuge in shelters. I have always been fortunate enough to have a roof over my head, even if I've been a little nomadic at times.

The early Brixton months were spent lodging with Marg whilst I found my feet before renting my own small flat nearby. That was on Brixton Hill and, being the busy thoroughfare that it is, I got coated in soot every time I opened the window. But it was the first place that I could call mine. Somewhere I lived without family, without flatmates, without a partner. Making me truly independent. I could so easily have stayed with Marg, but our relationship was in its infancy. This being her first relationship with a woman, she wasn't quite ready to cohabit and I had a lot of healing and reflecting to do. I felt that I had always run from one romantic situation into another and wanted to break that habit. Despite using Marg's utility room facilities, I needed to stand on my own two feet.

At 36, many people are established, married, have become parents and are determinedly settled. My years of being a butterfly, were perhaps now behind me. My parents had stood in my father's kitchen when I was about 15 or 16, I was seated at the table. "What are we going to do with her?", my mother had asked. "She can't be a butterfly all of her life. She needs stability." I don't recall my father's response, nor any reaction of my own, but butterfly was certainly an analogy that remained with me. One I found appropriate and that seemed to suit me more as the years passed.

In all the years I lived in London, I moved around a lot. Seemingly rootless. In and out of relationships that lasted some time, but which took me in and out of different homes. Had my wings eventually been clipped?

My arrival in London in 1978 had been a dream come true. Despite it taking a year longer than anticipated, it was to be my home for 25 years. A relationship so deep that once on a train journey home to Kent, I was prompted to make a note in my phone that, "As much as I love Kent I will always be in love with London." This prompted me to write a song about this special relationship called "You Do Me Good".

I had arrived in the capital city to attend the West London Institute of Higher Education (WLIHE, more commonly known as Borough Road Sports College). Incredibly substandard facilities for such a prestigious and aspirational seat of learning and sporting endeavour, even in the 1970s, but it was my base for 4 years. A place where I gained a Bachelor of Humanities Joint Honours Degree in Sports and Religious Studies – curious bedfellows, I know. Where I enjoyed the attentions and affections of several boyfriends and embarked on my first real-life, if closeted, same-sex relationship. Where I enjoyed accolades for my performances in front of hockey goals, partied hard, had a severe bout of glandular fever and eventually managed to acquire my degree. They were good days. Confusing at times. Tough at times. But a hell of a lot of fun. Throughout those 4 years, I lived in halls of residences, decidedly squalid shared houses and bedsits. And I bunked up in the flats of kindly and sympathetic friends when I fell foul of my own impulses or those of another.

At the same time that I was starting my first job, I moved to Southfields to share a house with an old family friend. A real house. It felt very grown up and like a proper home. My room was small, but I turned it into my own. I painted it in bright blues, yellows and black. Even the light switches were a rather fetching matt black and I had a somewhat revolutionary dimmer switch that caused great excitement. These were found and fitted for me by one of my oldest and dearest friends who I had met in a pub on the Strand. I was there after work with my then Canadian girlfriend, a punk. He had taken a shine to her, not realising the nature of our relationship. Sadly, for him, he got landed sitting next to me whilst his mate chatted her up. Luckily, we got on famously. I was even the best "person" at his subsequent marriage. That caused a stir in the Church of St John the Baptist in Malden. But in Southfields I found some security. Amongst the more memorable times, was a dinner party held for a small group of ladies befriended mainly at the Gateways, the legendary lesbian club made famous in the film, *The Killing of Sister George*. My aforementioned male friend decked himself in tails and served us drinks and a fine meal. I dressed in a bow tie and tuxedo that Radcliffe Hall would have been proud of. Personalised, embossed matchbooks, silver cigarette holder dripping from my mouth, silk handkerchief hanging from my top pocket.

This was during the time that the IRA were carrying out bombings in London and there were several occasions when I got too close for comfort. Travelling up to London from Southfields, one Saturday before Christmas to shop in Knightsbridge, I got as far as Putney Bridge and thought better of it. I am not a fan of department stores at any time but most especially not before Christmas. As I walked through the door, I heard the phone ringing.

"Oh, thank God," I heard Mum say.

"Why, Mum? What's happened?"

"There's been a bomb at Harrods. I wanted to check that you weren't there."

That evening I travelled up to see friends in north London and had to change trains a number of times because of suspicious packages. Life went on and we somehow became accustomed to the fear.

When the house in Southfields was put up for sale, I moved to a "born again" student flat in West Kensington. There were four of us in this apartment, which was very down at heel. Despite that, it had its own style and was the centre of fun, games, trials and tribulations. I lived first in the box room (that's probably a generous description – it was more of a broom cupboard, fortunately I like dens) but throughout my time there was gradually promoted by the resident landlady, matriarch and friend, to the pink room. Spacious, airy and very pink. One night, when she had resided in it herself and had consumed a fair quantity of Chardonnay, she took it upon herself to paint her room. The only colour she had was a powder pink. It covered every corner and piece of furniture.

I vividly recall sitting in the lounge there, in the summer of 1985, with the windows wide open and hearing Wembley Arena's televised Live Aid fundraising concert ringing out from every building across the courtyard.

Many nights after being out clubbing with "Auntie" – my girlfriend who was 20 years my senior, I squeezed into my box room. It was during this time that a furore erupted within my family about my sexuality. For the first time ever, aged 26, I had decided that I wanted to stay in London for Christmas to spend it with "Auntie". When I tried to explain this to my mother on the phone, she appeared not to understand what I was saying. "Mum, I think I'm going to stay in London this Christmas. I want to spend it with my girlfriend." There was a long pause, and then an unusually weak but emotionally charged voice on the other end of the phone. "I'm not sure I understand Jude. Are you trying to tell me something? Who else knows this? Am I the last to find out?" I wrote to her to explain. I then got a phone call (a completely rare event) from my father to tell me how distraught my mother was. She apparently had not realised that I had a strong preference for the fairer sex. She was shocked and terribly hurt about being the last to find out. I felt sure that I had been clear with her. There had been an evening when I was living in Southfields; I was under the influence and, feeling miserable because of my current relationship status, I had called her to pour out my troubles.

"Hi Mum. I thought I'd call," I said. "I haven't spoken to you for a while."

"Are you ok dear? You sound a bit wobbly," she replied.

"No, not really Mum," I sobbed. "My relationship has broken down."

"Oh dear, I'm sorry about that," she said. "I'm sure once you've had a good night's sleep you'll feel better. You're probably a bit overtired and emotional. Maybe no more wine tonight."

I rarely sought help from my mother but whose shoulder would you rather cry on than your mum's? It was a comfort to know that I had asked for help and had been given some reassurances by her and a relief to feel that I had revealed something of my true self to her. Perhaps I was incoherent, or she wasn't paying attention, or a combination of the two? Perhaps I wasn't explicit about my heart having been broken by a girl not a boy and had presumed other family members had set her straight. My father had certainly put two and two together a long time beforehand, although it wasn't something that we talked about. Or perhaps Mum wasn't wanting to hear what I was saying. The reality is very often that when you see something in writing it hits home rather more powerfully than in any other way. Which clearly it did a couple of years later. I ended up going home. Christmas was always fun at home but it hadn't been my first choice that year. Nothing more was said.

AIDS made itself known to us during this time. "Auntie" shared a flat with a number of people, including a wonderfully promiscuous young man, who I got on well with. He became very poorly, very quickly, as we were just becoming aware of this plague sweeping predominantly through the gay community. On one occasion when visiting him as I held his hand, he croaked through his oxygen mask, "When I get out of here, you and me are going dancing." Wishful thinking and positivity personified. He was dead before the week was out. I would never dance with him again.

Parties were a regular occurrence at West Kensington, as were evictions. The landlady had a habit of taking against her flatmates from time to time. There was no apparent reason for this nor when she famously Tippexed friends out of her address book. Somehow, I made it through, perhaps because I was very compliant and also valued our friendship, which was to continue well beyond our time sharing the same home. She was even responsible for bringing Marg and I together some years afterwards at her hen party. Although that hadn't been her intention, she found it a great source of amusement and entertainment. For a while at least. Ultimately, she did not approve and was very clear in expressing her new-found version of morality. Times had certainly changed.

My next stop was Tooting. There, I lived in a small flat with a new girlfriend, a cat and a parrot during a period of unemployment, having taken a stand at the Health Club I had been working at in South Kensington. From there and having found new employment at the big green store on the corner in Knightsbridge, I migrated to Shepherds Bush, to a flat owned and lived in by a consultant dermatologist friend of the West Kensington landlady. The soundtrack to my time there was Junior Walker and "How Sweet It Is" and Phil Collins and Philip Bailey singing "Easy Lover" on full pelt, using the consultant's serious sound system. I got locked in this flat one day, the day I was due to go to the wedding of my best buddy from college. How embarrassing. I'm not sure I've ever explained myself properly so if you're reading this, I am truly sorry and owe you.

The hurricane of 1987 took place in Shepherds Bush. It took place throughout the country in fact, but the remarkable thing for me was that night, the consultant was playing snooker at a club down the Goldhawk Road. He staggered home in the middle of it completely oblivious to the biblical scenes around him.

Then I went south again. To Forest Hill. And purchased a flat with my new (Australian) girlfriend. A lovely two-bedroom garden flat. You had to climb out of a window to get into the garden, but it still had one. One day, the developer who had converted the flat arrived on the doorstep complete with a gunshot wound to his eye. The weird thing was that we didn't blink at this. We found it a strangely jovial matter. Sadly, our time there was not to last. My girlfriend decided that she no longer wished to be in a relationship and would prefer for us to live together as friends. I dutifully moved into the spare bedroom. We had frank conversations and I asked her what would happen if I met someone else. This was her choice. And I did. She wasn't happy and literally begged on bended knee for me to stay. That she had changed her mind. Having your cake and eating it doesn't work out as a rule.

So, I moved myself and my possessions to South Norwood, to the home of my new amour. For 5 years, until circumstances put so much pressure on us that we crumbled. Laundry baskets flew. I fled. But not before I had gone to the hen party of the West Kensington friend and landlady. Where I met Marg. I don't tend towards corny, but I did spot her across a semi-crowded room and thought what a lovely, kind person she looked. I don't know whether it is reasonable to believe that you can read someone's personality from their face, but I believe that in this case I did and was right.

To her astonishment and bewilderment, I effectively wooed her. Finding an excuse one weekend to sneak away from the 'burbs of South Norwood to the somewhat grittier Brixton Hill. Complete with potato masher. Not being conversant in vegetarian cookery, I thought that the way to her heart may be garlic mash. With chopped chives and a drizzle of balsamic vinegar. I don't recall there being anything else. It appeared to work reasonably well although I suspect curiosity was the greater attraction for her.

Spending time there, and in my own rented flat down Brixton Hill, I masterfully managed rodent problems in her kitchen, decked out in my paint splattered blue dungarees and singlet in the days when I could see my biceps, and styled and decorated her flat including excessive use of Polyfiller and Mexican style steps in the garden. We swanned around in her silver dream machine, a stately Citroen DS, and took our first holidays together.

And then, after 2 years, we decided to buy our first home together. Off Brixton Hill around the corner in Hayter Road. A chunky, solid, safe and stylish terraced house. With a small but beautifully formed, walled garden, which we filled with fig and banana trees, bamboos and other glorious architectural plants. We have a photograph of my stepfather sitting underneath the banana tree with fruit bearing down on him looking rather regal, sheltering him from the sunshine.

We held many rather legendary parties in Hayter Road for friends and workmates. Vodka soaked melons exploded over the pavement to the sound of workmates' hysterical laughter. Scooter man booked to deliver friends and their cars home at the end of long, fun-filled evenings. Deciding to bleed radiators in our dining room minutes before ten friends arrived for ten courses of deliciousness on Millennium night. I broke my ankle badly here when I careered down the stairs with no shoes and socks on. It was the end of a murder mystery night organised for my team at work. After the accident, Marg left trays of wonderfully imaginative and loving food as I remained stranded as the one-legged wonder on our first floor. I got locked out one morning, in my black and white striped silk pyjamas, only to have a Polish builder use his ladder to somehow climb in through a small opening in our bathroom window to let me back in. I acquired my pride and joy of a Daihatsu Copen here only months before leaving and I drove the 5 miles to work in the City each day in it, taking me no less than 1.5 hours each way to do so. And we acquired a couple of beloved two-year-old feline brothers here. They then journeyed with us to our new (but very ramshackle old home) in the Kent countryside where they remained with us into their 20s. And to a new and very different life for us all.

Like a runaway train it goes moving on
Like a runaway train yes I'm going strong
I'm a runaway train rolling on and on
And I'm moving on, going home, going home.

Moving On

Kent

Sitting up in bed, feeling slightly under the weather and because I focus well here, I begin to write. A window is open and I can hear birds singing outside. The day is murky, that term that explains the slightly damp atmosphere following 2 days of rain. Autumn is approaching but I hope that some late summer sun will brighten the day. The temperatures are still mild and we venture towards the fire for evening comfort, rather than necessity.

Our bedroom is white. It is square. Our bed sits tidily in the middle of the wall. It seems to be holding court. Two doors: one of them opens onto the landing, the other into a small walk-in wardrobe. From the bed, I can see a toy monkey hanging on the door to the landing. It makes me chuckle because the previous night Marg said it looked like Jesus on the cross and was making her uncomfortable. It hangs alongside several strands of shiny beads.

I look straight ahead from behind my cosy, white duvet towards our dressing table: black lacquer supporting an ornate glass mirror, home to more baubles and several medals recognising Marg's triathlon exploits. Bottles of Chanel perfume, body lotion and shower gel. Bottles of sun tan lotion, nail varnish and a book about Man Ray in Paris.

Looking upwards and to the left are two artworks that look alike. One we bought many years ago on a visit to Kent. It is by Katie Saqui with the inscription, "Looking so beautiful, The Tide will come back in for more," on it. The other is a beautiful etching with gold leaf entitled, *Lines from San Carlo al Corso*, of that church by Mark Pulsford. They give me immense pleasure.

I have the radio on and stop writing for 15 minutes to listen to a reading from *In My Minds Eye* by Jan Morris. I have been a fan of Jan Morris since I read her book *Conundrum* when I was a teenager. A fabulous writer, and a fascinating and truly admirable human being. A couple of years ago, when visiting my father in Criccieth, North Wales, I popped into the local post office to pick up some pins for a cork board I had bought him. I turned around, whilst browsing the stationery, and spotted Jan Morris. I thought for a moment and then, not wanting the opportunity to pass me by, took a deep breath and said, "Please excuse me, but I just wanted to say hello and how much I have always admired you."

"Why, thank you so much," she said, then added charmingly, "That's very kind. I do hope we'll meet again." I read subsequently that for Jan, kindness and marmalade are two of the most important things in life. And from our brief encounter, I can certainly say that she practised the former.

I have spent a lot of time in this pleasingly uplifting, airy room over the last 8 years. I am hoping the current malaise is simply a slight seasonal lurgy. My natural way would be to ignore it and carry on, and then end up in bed anyway. But now, I reluctantly give in. I am learning that the sooner I give in, shake off a lurgy or allow my natural state to take its course, the sooner I will be back on my feet, recovered, with batteries restored.

Through the windows, I can see trees. Without lifting myself up, only trees. Below the low window is a burnished brown radiator. I commissioned all the radiators when we renovated and refurbished the house 13 years ago. On the wall above it are a pair of rectangular wall lights, which I spray painted in antique gold. I like a can of spray paint. In either corner, alongside the bed head behind me are Lloyd Loom armchairs in their original gold condition, untouched by me, bedecked in cast off clothing. On one, is a teddy bear bearing the hallmarks of being as old as I am and very originally named Teddy. I have left many things behind as I have made my way through life, but Teddy has stayed with me. To the left of the dressing table, a pair of Lloyd Loom laundry baskets. Gold satin and brown fur cushions are sprinkled around the room. Physical possessions are an interesting part of our lives. You can glean so much about people who live in a home by wandering through it. All the things that I have around me bring me comfort and make me happy.

I reflect on a drive home a few weeks previously. I had been away for 10 days. I alternated between singing along to a Glen Campbell playlist and listening to Spurs thrash Fulham on the radio. But regardless of that, I felt glad because I was going home and remembered our move to Kent, 14 years ago.

The day we moved to Kent was a very hot August day. I led the advance guard in my little beeper, my Daihatsu Copen, acquired just a few months before. A convertible, when the roof had folded neatly into the boot, there was no room for luggage.

Marg was bringing up the rear carrying two very disgruntled cats, Earl and Bertie, who were in their cages on the back seat of her Saab. I arrived first and sat on a bench admiring our new home, or ruin as it was at that time. Eventually, the removal men joined me, and beer and fags in hand we waited for Marg to arrive. Eventually, Marg and the cats appeared – on top of a breakdown truck. It had not been fun for Marg but we were united again and with so much to look forward to.

That evening, adopting the countryside ways and slower pace of life, we sat with old friends, feet up and glasses in hand, surveying what could only loosely be termed a garden at that stage. Nevertheless, it was magnificent, and bats swooped over our heads as we celebrated the day.

I had left a very good job. We had left a very good home. We had left London. I had left the familiarity of everything I had known, a home of 8 years, a company of 8 years and a city of a quarter of a century. Sometimes you take a deep breath and do things. Over thinking may mean you don't do them. I cast no judgement on those choices, but it doesn't tend to be my way. I can be an over thinker, a ruminator, a worrier. But I also have a fierce desire to gamble and step outside my comfort zone. Sometimes those two things clash. I don't know why I have this drive to do new things, but I'm sure I would have been a healthier, and possibly at times happier person, if it wasn't there.

We had been very measured when considering the move, even spending a week in a local hotel. But this was certainly a very big change and we were quite naïve in many ways. But naivety is sometimes necessary to enable change. It is sometimes not possible to be otherwise. That is one of the beauties of adventure. However much you plan and prepare, and think you've covered everything, there are likely to be things you just could not have anticipated.

And so, we stepped into the slightly unknown. We found out quite quickly that east Kent and most especially the east Kent countryside is not London. It is close to London. It is commutable. It has many inhabitants like us who have lived, worked and loved in London. It has many people who come down from London and buy second homes here, as we once considered doing ourselves.

We wanted to get away from the hustle and bustle, the sweet but rancid smells, the litter strewn pavements, the incessant sound of sirens and planes roaring overhead. We wanted to find a sense of calm among the orchards, hop fields and rolling downs. To be close to the many and varied seaside havens, to the sound of birdsong and big skies filled with stars at night. To smell clean air. To know slow food and kindly ways.

One of my abiding memories of the kindly ways outside of a big city was shopping in one of the Sainsbury's in Canterbury. I was taken aback because the lady on the checkout was so very pleasant. That may sound rather uninteresting but at the time it really did seem quite remarkable to me. No grunting. No lack of eye contact. No begrudging upturn of the corner of the mouth trained to tell us, "Have a nice day." A genuine smiling face, a sincere conversation, time taken to connect with a fellow human being.

The cats took to life in the country swimmingly. We had been told to secure them in their own room for several days and nights before allowing them to roam. The neighbour-free fields of Kent that wrapped around our new home were a far cry from the back-to-back gardens of urban Brixton. All sorts of things, including other creatures less tame and tolerant than they were used to, were waiting for them there. However, the morning after our first night we heard the creaking of a door and the gentle pitter-patter of paws along the landing before both boys leapt onto the bed for their good morning sniff. They remained happily and safely with us until very sadly Earl had to take his leave in 2013. Bertie, the scaredy-cat who had become Mr Sociable, died in 2017, aged 22.

The first few weeks saw a lot of plotting and planning. We made the house habitable for the forthcoming months, whilst we developed and researched a vision for our home. We met with architects who helped me develop our plans whilst Marg commuted into London each day for work, which at that time was as resources director for the British Council. In less than a year, the builders moved on site. By this time, we had dispensed with the services of the quantity surveyor. He had a habit of telling us that things weren't possible. Our architect would respond with, "All things are possible at a cost." A hopeful bunch. One thing I struggled with for many years after moving to Kent was this attitude. A slowness to respond, to get things done. Sometimes the lack of open mindedness and foresight. No sense of urgency. That is very much a generalisation, so please don't write in to complain. It isn't about right or wrong, but my own frustration having been used to a very different pace of life for so long. So, the quantity surveyor went and I became project manager as well as designer. Something of a learning curve: working up restructuring plans with our architect, commissioning just about everything that can be seen, co-designing bespoke wood-crafted kitchen units. Managing chippies, sparkies and builder bosses who had never attended a site meeting with an agenda. On one occasion when we were driving off for a long weekend, a flock of workmen descended around the car, "What do you want me to do about...?", "Jude are you contactable if …?", "There's a delivery arriving later today, where shall we put it …?" Oh, the feeling of empowerment as I turned left out of the drive. They could sort themselves out for a few days, couldn't they?

One of my favoured stories about the transformation of our home is recalling the very first day that the builders moved in. The first thing to be done was to erect a large shed. This would serve as a storage space for the clutter that was in a double garage due to be knocked down. The builder boss had instructed one of his men to be on site to receive the concrete slabs that would form the foundation for the shed. I had to go out for the morning. It all seemed in hand. The boss had reassured me that his man knew what to expect and what to do. I left him at 9.30am, sheltering from the sunshine under the shade of a tree with *The Sun* newspaper. I returned at 12.30pm, to find him sitting in exactly the same spot. With *The Sun*. Still doing the same crossword. "Have the slabs been delivered?", I asked, assuming he'd received them, stored them and was taking a lunch break before starting to lay them.

"No, they haven't arrived," he replied.

"Have you called them to find out where they are?", I asked.

"No, the house is locked, so I couldn't use a phone."

"And have you called your boss to tell him?"

"No, I don't use my own phone for work calls."

He had sat there poring over his crossword for 3 hours without questioning where the materials were or what he should do about the fact that they hadn't arrived. I didn't check to see if he had answered any of the clues. It was an ominous sign of things to come.

I've moved downstairs now and look outside. At the bottom of the front garden is a dinghy which lies unused, submerged under a tarpaulin and uncut grass. Not the original dinghy but one I picked up at a local charity shop, complete with mast which lies submerged somewhere in the shed. The original dinghy got stolen. It had been my ambition when we moved here to buy a wooden rowing boat for the pond which in many ways is more of a small lake – a natural pond that dries out in summer and refills in spring. I did get a dinghy built by a Whitstable smack boatbuilder. It was a thing of rare beauty. Crafted with immense pride and expertise. And it even had brass rollocks. My father was an incredibly talented craftsman. When I was young, he made things in his spare time and even built his own speedboat, which he raced competitively on the River Trent. Boats had played a part in my life and this was going to be something of a dream come true.

The theft of the beloved first dinghy was the stuff of a crime drama. It was tied up at the end of the decking that runs alongside the pond, tucked in underneath the willow. Covered up, and out of sight to anyone on the road or beyond, only visible to anyone who was to come on to our property. There had been a recent series of thefts of hedging plants, including our own.

During the week of the theft, Marg was staying in London for work and I had gone to stay with her. Unusually, both of our cars were overnighting at the station. It was springtime, the grass long and due for its first cut. The day after returning home, I was taking the bins down to the gate at the bottom of our drive, when something made me think of the boat which had lain dormant throughout winter. I turned towards the pond and realised it wasn't there. I knew for a fact that it had been there only a couple of days before, because I had ventured down to check the decking. There were no footprints or tracks in the long, damp grass which suggested that the only way the boat could have been taken was via the steep bank, fence and field to the side of the pond. The boat had been covered and full of water, making the solid wooden structure even more heavy. It would have taken several men to lift it. It seemed that someone knew it was there and watched for us to both be away from home. It was possibly opportunistic, but more likely planned. A sickening thought. We were angry. We were sad. We reported the theft to the police but there was little more that we could do.

For my sins, I was on the parish council at the time and the chair, an ex-police sergeant was so incensed that there was talk of a stake out. That would have been more of an Ealing comedy than Hollywood heist but nevertheless we did consider it. I was quite excited, but sadly we didn't follow through.

Despite its ominous start, the house was completed in June 2006. Builders had been on site for 10 months, not without incident. But the extraordinary place, which has now been our home for 14 years, was given a significant and deep makeover. Redesigned in places, a large and glorious kitchen extension, groundworks and landscaping, addressing the damp, rewiring, re-plumbing, reheating throughout. The fabric of this early 18th-century building was taken to task and the look and feel brought straight into the early 21st century. It was our very own grand design.

My love for interior design was not initially a conscious one. But even as a child I had shown a real interest in staging a room, in décor. My passion for building dens was perhaps a sign of my need to build nests. At college, I was asked to style others' rooms in halls. Wherever I lived, in whatever I lived, I made it a home; a place I felt proud of, happy to be in, happy to invite others into. So, when the decision was made for me to leave my job, along with us leaving London, it was decided that I would oversee the renovation of our new home. And that, ultimately, I would make interior design my new profession. Before the work started, I started a distance learning diploma in interior design with KLC School of Design in Chelsea Harbour. The course was shelved whilst our project was undertaken and resumed in the summer of 2006. I qualified with a respectable qualification in November 2008 and promptly went to R Soles on the Kings Road and bought myself an expensive pair of black, suede cowboy boots. I still wear them proudly to this day.

This was the year of the financial crisis. We lived in a location I was still unfamiliar with. I didn't know its habits, cultures and business practices. I found networking challenging, the pursuit of commissions and selling myself very uncomfortable, and so overall my freelance ambitions were not fruitful. I did a few small projects for people who were largely unwilling to invest in any level of expertise. I delivered some workshops but apart from our home, the largest project I did was for a friend in Brussels.

I started offering B&B in our contemporary, Indian-styled guest room. It has a hot pink rubber floor, satinate curtains, and a wall-hanging from Delhi. Vibrant colours of turquoise, greens and pinks combined with brilliant white, made it an enchanting space, as did the iridescent mosaic tiles in the en suite shower room. This was mainly a weekend business, but was well received. I added private dining to the offer and it went very well. I would have been very delighted to have stayed here as a guest. Not a money spinner because I only had one room and no way to increase capacity. But we enjoyed the company of some fascinating and fun people. My very first guests were a well-known journalist and her unofficial partner. Another intriguing guest was a golf agent attending the British Open in Sandwich. Very mysteriously, she entertained a gentleman friend who arrived late at night and left before dawn. Not every booking was so full of intrigue, but it offered solitude, special surroundings and safety for anyone needing to get away from prying eyes and for anyone just simply needing to relax and restore. Around this time, we also got hens. Two black rocks, Vita and Virginia, who were later joined by Gertrude and Alis. They provided us with the most golden of free range, organic eggs and hours of entertainment wandering around outside, tapping on the windows, waddling in and out of the kitchen.

Andy Warhol stated that, "The world fascinates me." Well, people fascinate me. Apart from the rich vein of characters who passed through our door and guest room as B&B guests, I was – as I said – a member of the parish council. I maintain that I was slightly put up to this, but I won't hold anyone responsible – publicly. The main thing I would like to draw attention to with regards the parish council, is that we can be very quick to judge people. We all do it. It is human nature to make assumptions. It's important to try not to judge based on those assumptions. And to be open to the realisation that we may be very wrong. I used to attend parish council meetings and sit there thinking, "What am I doing? I have not a jot in common with almost anyone around this table." My yardstick was: would I go for a drink with anyone here? I actually found myself getting quite stressed about it at times. And then I called a meeting of the communications sub-committee, to be held at our home, and invited all of the council members to come for a drink afterwards. And how worthwhile that proved to be. A small band of us stood around in our kitchen, politely swigging our glasses of wine or cordial. And gradually, it evolved through conversation, that in actual fact most of us had an enormous amount in common. In our case it was music. The most unlikely members had been session musicians for Manfred Mann and Cat Stevens. Another's deceased husband had been a jazz aficionado, frequenting the jazz haunts of Soho in the 1960s. She still had a cellar full of musical mementoes and LPs. I had recently started singing in public aged 50. I was almost awestruck. I certainly felt very humbled. How wrong can we be?

Many good times have been had in our kitchen. We used to hold an annual bonfire party and would open our bifold doors from the kitchen onto the terrace. My band, Jude and the Obscures, would play live music inside as fireworks exploded from beside the pond. We have held dinner parties in it when numbers grew too big for our cosy dining room. We have attached marquees to it for bigger celebrations, such as my 50th birthday party in 2009 and our glorious Spanish themed Love Fest Wedding Party in early June 2015 which, saw people camping in the garden, eating paella, dancing to live music and revelling in the early summer sunshine. The most idyllic of days.

This home has been a place of celebration and a refuge. When my health deteriorated in 2010, and I was diagnosed with M.E., little did we know to what extent. Requiring solitude, peace and nature, it was the best place I could find myself. The house is in need of some restoration now. After 14 years we are moving through it slowly giving it the TLC it needs and deserves. At some stage, not too far away, it will be time to allow someone else to tend to it and relish it in the way that we have. It will be time for us to move on to pastures new. It will be time to revel in the experiences that a new home can bring for the next chapter of our lives.

Graduation Day

Gowns and glad rags
Expectation in the air
Pints being downed outside the cathedral,
Weather fair.

Tensions running high
Proud parents wondering what
Will become of their little children
All dressed up and looking fine.

People floating round waiting to go in
To receive what could be their passports
To ambitions,
Success therein.

High heels, swishy dresses,
Awkward suits and bushy beards.
The freshers looking on questioning their own fate,
Chatting in the cafes trying to work out who's their mate.

Romances soon to blossom,
Heartaches still to come.
Standing on their own two feet,
Until they run to Mum.

The world is now their oyster,
Will they take the reins and fly,
Take advantage of all that's offered,
Or hang their heads and cry.

So much to learn and find out,
Embarrassments and joys,
Do they stick to what they know
Or try out girls and boys.

Maybe one day they'll be invited back
To walk up the aisle inside,
The cathedral holding its breath
As you are paraded there with pride.

Your very own trumpet voluntary
The heads turn to see you stride
Taking your place amongst the dignitaries
Calm, deserving, glorified.

Your very own coronation,
Head held up high and bold,
The congregation look on in awe
As your story it is told.

You speak so very impressively,
Give the younger ones your message,
"Go out into the world, be wise, be tolerant, fair.
Be kind, work hard, be satisfied.
Whatever the colour of your hair.

Then when you've let your dreams take flight,
When you end your days of adventure
You can rest assured you'll have done your best
Knowing you've done by the world what's right
You've contributed across divides.

(I was inspired to write this when standing in the centre of Canterbury near the Cathedral in the summer of 2018, watching the Kent University graduates gathering on their big day. I then thought of Marg who had been one of them over 30 years before, and how she had returned to receive an honorary doctorate in 2015. The two scenes morphed into each other. In her speech on that momentous day she talked about crossing divides.)

"But it was fine at 8 am" – a journey into King's Wood

(King's Wood is a 1500-acre forest in the Kent Downs Area of Outstanding Natural Beauty, in Challock. It is managed for conservation, recreation and timber production, and is open to the public throughout the year. King's Wood was historically a royal hunting forest and a large herd of fallow deer still run free in the wood and since 1994 artists have been commissioned to make sculptures within the forest and also other kinds of artworks.)

Tramping into the wood, blue sky's turning rapidly grey. Rain drops falling, heavily now. "You cannot be serious", "I don't believe it" spring to mind. It isn't spring yet despite the daffodils' best efforts.

Muddy, the paths could do with more flint.

I listen for sounds of nature but hear traffic. Let's go deep into the wood and leave that perpetual buzz behind. I thought I'd left London.

Trees stand ahead of me like bristles on the back of a hedgehog.

Bits of rubbish on a wide-open space. Where are the bins? Why don't people take it home with them?

Mole holes. They've found this place too.

Young trees or dogwood? A mass of autumnal rusts remain here. A no. 2 haircut – very neat.

More flint underfoot – safer.

Green grasses that didn't turn brown looking like samphire.

Let's take the short cut.

Trees young and old, tall and short, the track opens up, well, widens.

A duathlon here on Sunday – I should be marshalling – don't envy them on bikes down these muddy slopes.

Going a way I've not gone before passed gnarled trees-tree chaos.

I set out at 9am. Exhilarating expectations and sensations of sunshine and wind but got rain – a lot of it.

Warm and dry in my "tent" of waterproof clothing. I walk through a wide opening – a mixture of life – young spruces sprouting to one side (not sure what they actually are but it felt good saying it) and on the other side trees ravaged by time and the elements. A world and a wood of contrasts.

Onwards.

Aha. The blue sky breaks through again.

Trees standing tall and proud on a bank – the sun sometimes casting shadows. The gentle patter of raindrops descending from on high.

Golden browns pierced by patches of green in between.

The sound of a bird, a pheasant, an escapee from the shoot. Turn right to avoid the steep hill ahead, off piste and further into the wood.

What do I find? A hole in the ground – nothing finer. (Than a score for.)

Sit beside a cloud and drink it in. A wet wood – puddles and pools, no mushrooms no stools (apart from the odd dog's.)

A large raindrop smacks me on the back and wakes me from my reverie.

Now for tea … fiddle dee dee.

It turned out to be coffee. The dandelion variety. Very natural and healthy especially with rice milk.

Sun to the left, trees to the right. Leaves and mud on the ground. Leaning against a log hut. Good fire wood. Fungus grows freely. Can still hear the distant traffic, and the hoot of a train.

A gentle wind finds its way through then subsides. Plink, plonk of the raindrops working their way through the branches.

Slip, slide to the musical installation. Paul Simon meets the Pogues.

With no one else around and plenty of water to feed it there are plentiful sounds. Now I must be homeward bound.

I rise gently over sodden leaves and rivers of mud, finding my way around stumps and nature's debris, hints of a new year dawning as tender shoots burst through.

Vibrant moss covers the remains of an old tree–a forest in itself. Fungus like oyster shells, solid to the sight but soft to the touch.

The cloud chamber from above looks like a wig cut badly, hacked.

Distant thumps like someone dropping heavenly boxes from a great height- no planes on a reccie from Lydd today – trees creaking as they sway to and fro. The constant hum of traffic.

Squelch, squelch as I plod along.

Nature calls. Did I, didn't I? Only I will ever know. Unless the trees have ears as some of them surely do.

Splash, splash as down I go to civilisation as I know.

Into a leafy glade, an enchanted forest.

As I stumble across circle, line, stone the wind blows up, the rain comes for me. Trees resemble the leaning tower of Pisa. Distant rumbles-thunder?

Trees chopped down, branches still strewn on the ground as though savaged by a hurricane.

Wingle, wangle, watch my footing.

The sound of birds trilling – where are you? Show yourselves.

I imagine a brace of game popping up in front of me (one for me, one for you) but no. Dreaming again. Must be getting tired. Go towards those damn cars.

Past the Wicker Bowl and the stage for the B52's-what did they sing? Anyway where is it's tail? Overgrown. It needs a cut.

On, on, on I go merrily (and wearily) on my way.

Stunning old yew. Branches bursting forth.

Traffic. Terra firma.

THE END

Potholes

Parish council, pot holes, pot holes.
Overgrown verges, pot holes, pot holes.
Fiery conversation filling up spaces,
Sniggers round the table, communications.

Parish council, pot holes, pot holes.
Planning, conservation, pot holes, pot holes.
Christmas Tree lights on, revolutionary applications,
Crisis in the country, descending into hades.

Parish council, pot holes, pot holes.
Summer fete runs smoothly, pot holes, pot holes,
Don't make assumptions behind blank faces,
You've so much in common, if not communal faces.

Travel

Welsh Rarebit

During my finals year at college, I managed to get a very serious dose of glandular fever. After being shipped home and seeing out the remainder of my third year there, I was eventually sent off to various relatives to convalesce. The most wonderful of these experiences was to stay in Manorbier in Wales with my beloved aunt and godmother, and my uncle. My home with them was a wonderful, large and double-fronted house set in beautifully tended gardens with a sweeping staircase down into the hall leading out to a paved walkway with a perfectly, centrally located fishpond as its feature. Apart from the bats that came in through the open front door as my uncle gardened until 1am, I enjoy memories of my aunt and I sharing many deep and meaningful conversations. We would continue to do this on subsequent occasions, sharing too glasses of red wine and cigarettes as we chewed over life. She wasn't afraid to talk honestly and openly to me about her own feelings and life, nor to ask me about mine. One of those candid conversations involved her bowing her head rather sheepishly and with a mischievous grin but kind and twinkling eye, asking, "Who's the boy in your relationship?" It was a question thrown at me about my current girlfriend. "Well it doesn't really work like that, Auntie," I replied. "You don't have to role play any more than two heterosexual people or two boys may do." She and I then delved more deeply into the subject. For some people, whatever their gender or sexual persuasion, role-playing may be their thing. I actually prefer not to focus on people's sexual proclivities. It is of no special interest to me. When I explained that to her, it resulted in a good and meaty conversation. "You little blessing," she said as we wrapped up that chat. I love that she was bothered and brave enough to speak of such things and I miss her to this day. I remember the night she knocked tentatively on my bedroom door late at night. She had come to ask for sympathy after she had slipped going out of the front door, landing legs akimbo in the pond. She, of really very ample proportions, had ripped her stockings and bruised her legs and her pride, but how we laughed. "You little bugger," she said, her tears of sorrow turning to joy as I stifled snorts and giggles and we fell across the bed in fits of laughter. No one could have pulled that off if they had staged it.

Beauty of youth, glistening and glowing
So much to prove - ego's everything.
Beauty of youth, perceived perfection.
Frightened the truth will mean rejection.

Beauty of Youth

Jobs

"Every goal you reach begins with the decision to start."

I'm not sure who that can be attributed to, but it sits on the wall at the bottom of some steps leading up to a studio. A gym. One that I went to for a few months last year. Just once a week, if it was possible. As a health practitioner, I've used over the last 8 years, said to me at the end of last year, "You need to use twice as much energy to do half as much work, any work, any activity." This was still the main challenge for me. My recovery from M.E. had been good, and I had felt that the time was now right to focus not only on my health but a gradual restoration of some fitness once again.

I had made my start.

Gyms have been an integral part in my life. I started using one aged 18 and although I had to stop aged 53, they have played a prominent part in my personal and professional life.

It was when I was in sixth form and using a small health club in my hometown that I formed an attachment to them. I was playing a lot of hockey and my stepfather-to-be suggested I might enjoy it. I more than enjoyed it. It is fair to say that it became an obsession. It also instilled in me a desire to work in health clubs.

I wasn't ever a typically sports-crazy person. I enjoyed watching sports and taking part in some and happened to be quite good at one or two. For this reason, a Joint Honours Degree including Sports Studies was more a means to an end, rather than an opportunity to indulge any hobbies. I had a keen interest in nutrition and at college, studied sports psychology and sociology. I found these to be big and interesting subjects and I was looking forward to applying them to a working environment. The artist Jeremy Deller said that he sometimes finds sport pompous. I get that. Egos and competitive spirits can very easily morph into pomposity. In fact, to get away from that a little and to satisfy a creative need, I included a contemporary dance module as part of my own studies.

The reality is that in the 1970s and 1980s there wasn't a fitness industry as we know it today. Health clubs were quite rare. The one I had gone to initially was a small room with a couple of bikes and some free weights, as well as an instructor with a questionable ability to instruct. And a sauna. When asked by one of his daughters what he did when he went to the gym, my stepfather would reply, "I spend half an hour in the sauna." Needless leg pulling would follow but I'm sure his time in the sauna contributed a lot to his exercise routine and came with many health benefits. The alternative to such establishments then was makeshift spaces where blokes pumped iron in skimpy vests and baggy pants, grunting and grinding, heads raised high seeking a sense of glory, testosterone flying. With very few health benefits.

Smitten by the prospect of working in health clubs for a living, I got a place to do a sports studies degree, having retaken an A level to make sure I could go. I had chosen one of the top two colleges in the country, the West London Institute of Higher Education, (Borough Road College), over Loughborough because of the latter's more exacting academic standards and because I was eager to go to London. I had still set my bar high and getting over that bar may not always be straight forward, as I was often to find out, but I have always been relentless in believing that goals are achievable in the end.

And so, the girl for whom fitness regimes had become an integral part of her life went to college. Until the year earlier, when she should have entered this pantheon of athleticism in West London, it was almost solely the domain of glistening, glowing, fit and talented young men. Gifted in the arts of rugby, football, athletics. Entry was via two A levels, a minimum of county standard in one sport, an interview and physical tests.

When the time came for her to attend, it was as part of a small band of eleven girls embarking upon life in this previously male bastion in the leafy suburbs of Isleworth. It was the late summer of 1978. A time initially of a lot of fitness training, running around the track religiously each evening to maintain the weight loss she had achieved before arriving there. A lot of fun, frivolity, lifelong (if interrupted at times) friendships, fierce competition, sporting fulfilment and academic activity in a limited fashion filled her time. Delayed again in achieving her academic awards this time due to glandular fever, she eventually qualified in 1982.

A stint in the clinical supply department at Kingston Hospital in West London, dancing at the Christmas party to the strains of "Come On Eileen" filled a gap in employment terms whilst the search went on for what would become the first rung on her career ladder.

Westminster Gym

That chance came when I applied successfully to a company called Fitness for Industry (FFI) in February 1983. A row of four, suited and booted men faced me across the table at my interview, each of them bearing the hallmarks of the military careers they had known. I was invited to attend a month-long and very intensive training course with them before being placed in the Westminster Gym to assist someone who had been one of my interviewers, in running that small, not-for-profit facility. A gym open to all inmates of the Palace of Westminster, it was located at that time in a carpeted room on the fourth floor of the Norman Shaw North building. My boss had wanted to give me the job because I had laughed a lot in the interview and thought we would have fun working together. A former physical training instructor in the Paras and a father figure in part during my time working with him. He taught me so much. And we did have a lot of fun.

This was a fascinating time full of incredibly rich experiences. It was a huge privilege to be given the opportunity to exist in the world of Westminster – a bubble full of intrigue, innuendo, angst and impending action – a place that kept its own hours. The seat of power where many of the leading lights, and slightly more shadowy characters, were able to avail themselves of, in most cases, some much needed leisure time, exercise and relaxation for their stressed minds and bodies in the small oasis that I inhabited. Chock full of characters they came to be assessed and to do their best to improve their health and that of the nation.

Fitness for Industry was very much ahead of its time. Their levels of professionalism remained with me throughout my career in the health and fitness industry; their standards recognisable in future places of employment amongst colleagues who had been schooled in their methods and disciplines. Maybe borne of the military but ones we were all proud to maintain.

Fitness assessments were rigorous for all potential gym members. Cycle tests had them wired up to heart monitors, blood pressure was taken, height and weight measured, strength tests and lung capacity analysed. And there were GP referrals for anyone falling below the safe guidelines stipulated. Impressive in their attention to detail, these measures saved at least one person who went on to have a quadruple bypass as a result of our findings and assisted many, through the accuracy of their outcomes, enabling staff to provide properly tailored exercise programmes, which I regret to say that I don't think I saw the likes of again once commercialism became the byword and lip service only was paid to preventive medicine.

Members from both houses, security staff and the press attended. Memorable moments at every turn. People jumping from my television screen into my day-to-day life in person. Being introduced to an army major. Putting my hand out to shake his only to be presented with a hook. The Minister for Northern Ireland's bodyguard coming in one day and handing me his gun to put away for safekeeping. How safe it was in the unlocked draw of our rickety wooden desk in the cupboard without a door that was our office, I don't know. Spending too much time late at night in the Lords' Bar, rising at the crack of dawn to open the gym doors at 6am, looking out of the train window at the glorious sunrises over London as I made my way across the Thames for those early starts. Taking a nap under the desk of the leader of Plaid Cymru because a mate worked for him, before it all started again. Waiting for taxis at the end of those evenings and have my partners in crime berating eminent Scottish Tory MPs wearing kilts. Silly, but we amused ourselves no end with such pranks. Being interviewed for a BBC South programme along with a dynamic young Tory MP, the camera panning to a long shot of his slight but upright stature, with his foppish blonde curly hair and beard, leaving the gym revealing bowler, brolly and boxer shorts. Assessing a prominent private secretary shortly before the story about her affair with an even more prominent cabinet minister and their forthcoming love child broke. Privacy and confidentiality without question. Demonstrations of respect and dignity always. This was a place where stories could have broken every day but for those things, learning very quickly how you had to play the game and the value of integrity. "Do unto others as you would have them do to you." Something I learned the meaning of there and which has stayed with me throughout my life, however much people or situations have tried to test it.

And something did come to test it quite quickly. After about 18 months in post as assistant manager my boss was going to be transferred to run the FFI facility at the Grosvenor House Hotel. A great move for him with far more responsibility. Not unreasonably he recommended that I should take over from him and a replacement be found for me.

The Westminster Gym was unusual as FFI facilities went because it had its own committee full of MPs and lords who governed decisions about policy. A band of middle aged, more than middle class, white Tories who rather blatantly didn't feel that this young filly was capable of leadership. These being the Maggie Thatcher years, the Iron Lady had clearly not convinced them that women were capable. Unhesitatingly and swiftly they rejected his recommendation. Every effort seemed to be made to find an alternative to appointing me as the manager, which caused an uproar in this hotbed of politics. Not least with two women who had become two of the best friends I would ever make in life and remain so to this day, despite one departing this world a couple of years ago. She remains with us in spirit, believe me! Feisty feminists both, they set about campaigning to reverse the decision.

Petitions were drawn up. I was at the head of the Women's Committee Agenda. An up and coming female Labour MP who went on to achieve great things (apart from becoming the leader of her party) paid her £100 membership fee so that she could say she was a member of the gym and sign the petition. But the Tories were not for turning. I kept my head down, was grateful for the extraordinary levels of support I was given and in due course a young man straight out of occupational therapy college was brought in as my boss. I taught him his job, showed him the ropes and was rewarded by his gratitude and humility as my co-worker. Fortunately, he was not of the same stock as our masters and we got on famously until the time came in the summer of 1984 for me too to be moved on.

I look back on this and try to recall the impact it had on me. I was only a girl really. Embarking upon a promising career. Still working her way through the twists and turns of an exciting but mostly complicated personal life. One that made her feel obliged to live a double life at times.

These were the days when homosexuality was legal but frowned upon, not welcomed nor acknowledged by the general populous. And coming out was certainly unlikely to enhance your career prospects. Even if you were sure you wanted to. This girl wasn't sure she wanted to yet. There was still a lot to be explored and worked out. She had no steady girlfriend nor boyfriend. She didn't and doesn't believe you have to confine yourself to one thing or the other. It becomes complicated more because of the restrictions that society places on us, what we grow up to believe is acceptable or not and feeling forced to choose. By nature a worrier, concerned about what other people think, being afraid of offending people, made things harder to manage. And so, she didn't reveal her true self in case people thought poorly of her and for fear of the repercussions. She had recently weathered a very complicated and closeted love affair with a woman. Then her heart was broken whilst she had remained a loyal and supportive friend to that person. She had flings with men too but was mostly interested in just enjoying life to the full either through work, or socially with those mates who knew the real her. Just wanting to live her life freely in the way that most do in their early 20s. I wonder if she sometimes used this to mask any pain she felt about the personal dilemmas and heartaches? Partying often into the early hours, driving herself through her days work on little sleep. Perhaps it was not surprising that she chose to keep her head down. Sticking her head above the parapet, even though at times she wanted to, was not her natural style and there were plenty of willing volunteers doing that on her behalf particularly during this difficult time. She knew that to have done so may have made her professional position more fragile and her lifestyle more exposed. Heaven knows what would have happened had the powers that be known that she was gay as well as a woman.

She sought advice confidentially from a trusted uncle. He was a GP in practice with her father and a liberal minded Justice of the Peace. He was the only family member she sought advice from, perhaps feeling some uncalled-for degree of shame. This wasn't something of her making. She was the victim of circumstance and the bigotry of others. She acted on her uncle's advice to ride this one out, let the support of others carry her through and relied upon his words, "You will come out of this with the greater respect of others than if you jump up and down and cause a stir, which may ultimately cause you greater trouble."

That advice she would always return to when confronted by challenging situations in the future and when the temptation to go into battle reared its head. It was a time that would go down in her history as a harsh and immense life experience, perhaps not to be repeated but certainly administering strength of character and a whiff of the harsh reality of life. She wonders sometimes how different life might have been had she chosen to go into battle, taken a more prominent stand against the injustices of this world. To dive into conflict was not something she relished. Was the way she chose to deal with things, being a keeper of the peace, actually a good or bad thing for herself and others? Perhaps it is not too late for her to turn.

Leaving the Westminster Gym was not going to be done quietly though. A party of generous proportions was organised for me. I don't think I have ever felt quite so feted since and I have enjoyed some glorious celebrations. The gym was cleared. Food and drink shipped in. Members packed the room. Gifts were given. Amazing mementoes of a time well spent. At the end of the evening a handful of the members, my boss and I peeled off and carried on with our partying into the night. Staggering through the streets of London, we were eventually down to three. Arm in arm we went, for support but as comrades chuckling as only late-night revellers can do with sheer joy and pride in the drunken escapades of the evening. Tottering along, tittering happily, arriving somehow at the door of an unsuspecting friend. We were somewhere in Pimlico. It was 2am. Hammering gently, whispering oh-so-loudly between sniggers until a head appeared at an upstairs window asking, "What the hell are you doing?", "We need a floor for the night and we can't get home. That okay?", "Sure come on in, I won't be a sec." The door opened and we three tumbled into her front room, where we had a double sleeping bag and some cushions thrown at us and as carefully as we could squeezed into it together for what remained of our night. Suppressed and satisfied snorts sending us to our slumbers.

Naturally (and hopefully) after a night like that there is a morning the next day. I went as arranged, but in a pretty sorry state, to visit my new place of work on the Strand before making my way back to Westminster where I was due to attend a luncheon given by the Speaker of the House of Commons and as the guest of a political commentator (now BBC deputy editor). A more charming man you could not hope to meet. I didn't read anything more into this than it being his leaving gift to me, nothing more than a friendly gesture and one I was honoured to accept. I enjoyed the company of men as I have always done, many of my best friends being men to this day, and I enjoyed having boyfriends from time to time despite other parts of my life remaining a closed book to most.

The time arrived for our lunch date. I stood patiently outside the tube station wondering how long I could stay there before believing it polite to absent myself, wondering indeed how long I could actually continue standing. Big Ben had struck 12, which was the appointed time for our assignation. Big Ben struck 12.15. He duly arrived apologising profusely for being late. My heart sank. My heart rate went up. We continued to the luncheon. In the heart of the palace. Long tables, silver service, fine linens, fusty people. We were seated and lunch was served. Melon with glace cherries never a favourite. Grilled trout swimming in butter. And trifle. I excused myself to pay a visit to the ladies. When I returned, having toyed with the first two courses and requesting a coke instead of wine I had to relent and leave my pudding. "You look a little peaky dear," commented the kindly waitress. "Oh, I just have a small appetite. It was all really very lovely, thank you," I uttered through dry lips and a spinning head. The lunch was over after some speeches and in a blur I thanked my host and hot footed it for my train. I'm not sure that I have ever felt that anyone was so deserving of an apology as that man. If he should ever get to read this, I would like to say how sorry I have always been for being such a lousy lunch guest.

Luxury in South Kensington

Within a year of running another small gym for FFI, my first boss at the Westminster Gym, headhunted me to go and join him in a new venture in South Kensington where he would be setting up a high-end health club for a hotel chain. I jumped at the chance. There would be two assistant managers, I would be running the health and fitness side of things and another young woman was running the front of house operation. On top of that, I would have input into the décor. No expense would be spared and I was able to appoint my own team and take on far more responsibility. The club is still there. Having passed it many times since, I ventured in a year or two ago and nothing much had changed. With echoes of a Roman spa, the only thing that appeared to have been replaced was the hand-painted mural that had covered an entire wall alongside the luxuriant bar area. It had the names of all of the staff subtly stencilled into the picture. I'd had my input into the design and décor – a heaven-sent situation for me. My first real foray, and the only one for a long time, into any professional world of interior design. I did appoint my own team.

Things were going very well until I found out that my fellow assistant manager, who in reality had fewer responsibilities than me, was earning considerably more. And so I resigned. A difficult and devastating decision, I left on amicable terms. But the man I had respected from the day I met him, who I had laughed with, confided in, whose values I thought I shared, had let me down immeasurably. In these circumstances, I accept that you do have to put things in perspective. Perhaps resigning was quite a radical choice coming so soon after being at the centre of some very blatant discrimination in my first job. I had ridden that out as graciously as I possibly could and didn't feel able to do so again even if the losses for me would be great.

Recent events have brought this seemingly eternal problem very much to the fore. Whilst listening to a fabulous *Fortunately* podcast brought to us by Fi Glover and Jane Garvey (both deserving of honours in my view for the delights they bring us across the airwaves), their guest in one episode, Susanna Reid, introduced the subject of equality and pay.

When alluding to some difficulties of her own at work with a male colleague she referred to people who had said, "You should for the sake of your own dignity just walk." But to her it hadn't made any sense that it should be her who felt forced to. Jane Garvey concurred by stating that it tended to be the woman, in cases where the issue might be between a man and a woman working together, who would have to part with their living. So here we have the issue of sexual inequality on a very basic level. Susanna Reid went on to expand on this highlighting that inequality isn't always between men and women but could also be between people of the same sex, which is what made me really sit up and pay attention.

The debate surrounding pay gaps is a deeply uncomfortable one. According to Susanna Reid, "It's put a lot of pressure on individual women to talk about it, to disclose." In her opinion, people should not feel obliged to discuss it and that it is the responsibility of an employer not an individual to disclose. I agree.

My reasons for leaving my job in South Kensington was not an example of a gender pay gap gripe. It was an example of inequality between two people of the same gender supposedly employed on an equal footing. It was also an example of a lack of transparency and honesty. It is my belief that it was not my responsibility nor that of my fellow assistant manager to share the knowledge of our earnings, although in fact I think it was from her that I found out. She was as innocent in this duplicitous act as I was. Our boss was not. Perhaps he was under pressure himself? This was not a tactic for pushing anyone out. He knew full well what we both earned and either wrongly thought it acceptable to pay us different amounts and/or naively thought he would get away with keeping it quiet. Whatever his motives the actions he took regarding this particular situation did us all a huge injustice.

My perception of these cases is that my fellow manager was offered more money because she asked for it when she was interviewed. Perfectly reasonable. They wanted to bag her and possibly thought nothing of the fact that that made things unequal. If they considered her worthy of more money that is the point where transparency should have come into play but of course didn't and still doesn't so often. Because they can get away with it and keep costs down? Because fairness isn't important in a commercial world? Just because.

I did come out of this with the losses. I had made my point but I hadn't gained anything. I had done what Susanna Reid said we shouldn't do. I had walked for the sake of my dignity. I had lost my living. I was unemployed for a year without any benefits because leaving my job had been my choice. I tried to set up some personal training on a self-employed basis and travelled from Tooting in South London up to Royal Oak in the West to work in a gym a few evenings a week for someone I had known at college. To say it was not an easy ride is an understatement.

In parallel with this, personally I had been floating on a sea of self-doubt, angst and adrenaline where my sexuality was concerned. The highs and lows of a still or stormy ocean tossing and tipping me one way and then another. I followed my heart because that's your one real chance for truth and happiness. I had by now realised that women would be my world romantically. I had bounced from one relationship to the next during this turbulent professional time. Strutting my stuff with friends and girlfriends at underground gay and lesbian clubs. The infamous Gateways, was a regular Friday and Saturday night destination. The Ace of Clubs in Piccadilly, which partly inspired the title track for my first album, This Girl, This Woman, often being the choice of venue to move on to on a Saturday. Crazy Larry's on a Sunday. Dressing to kill in sassy tuxedos with monogrammed silk handkerchiefs and New Romantics hair. Giving it my all on the dance floors in my patent pointy shoes, egged on by friends with whom I shared so many incredibly crazy but happy times.

Harrods

A break came for me professionally, when I landed a new job working for the UK suppliers of a brand of fitness equipment as their consultant at Harrods. I served some lovely people, got to visit some very celebrated homes to set up their equipment and train them, including one actress I remember vividly. She had extreme halitosis.

During this time, a person who made a truly significant impression on me and who became a firm friend until her untimely death only a short time after I left Harrods, was a singing star of the 1950s. She was also in occasional films such as *Cockleshell Heroes*, her star having faded with the advent of pop music. To earn her keep, she graced us with her presence, professionalism and her enduring glamour each day where she came to run the Slendertone concession from her sauna hut in the fitness equipment department. An actual pine wooden sauna that smartly housed a treatment room. *Are You Being Served?* had nothing on this. Her Majesty would process out of her hut each morning having dispensed with her trademark cape, figure trim and upright, dazzlingly smart two-piece suit, high heels, blonde hair in an elegant bun. With lippy and a smile fixed, she would announce regally to we young whippersnappers, "Darlings we are on stage, let the show commence," as the store's opening bell rang out. I have always tried to remember her sage words even at times when going out on whatever my stage might be was the last thing I felt like doing. Remembering her always brings a smile to my face.

What a woman. Generous with her time, her fags, her honesty when sharing her concerns about the difficulty she was having swallowing, a brandy and rum supply kept in her hospital bedside cabinet for her guests when she had become very poorly, and her extremely wicked sense of humour. She had me sussed from the moment she met me. She was a woman of the world not to be conned by my references to my "flatmate", in fact my Australian girlfriend.

We cross paths with people in so many ways: at work, through friends, in bars, in nightclubs, as strangers whose eyes may meet across a room or even a street. With enough practice this can become an especially useful tool when you exist partially in an underworld. What type of relationship you form with each of them depends on chemistry, opportunity, alcohol sometimes, how bold you may be with or without stimulants. Those relationships may be fleeting, they may be longer lasting. This flatmate was the first person I bought a property with. She had never had a girlfriend before and only a year into our time together, decided she wanted our relationship to be platonic. I removed myself and my belongings to our spare bedroom. I'm not sure why it was me who moved but I did. We discussed the situation like grown-ups, "I understand. Really I do. It's all too much too soon. We can see how things go. But have you thought about what happens if I meet someone else in time?", I had to ask. "That's okay. I'll understand if that happens," she replied. In due course, I did. She didn't understand and begged me on bended knee to reconsider. It was a sorry end. She returned to Australia, we gave the flat back as I couldn't maintain the upkeep on my own, and that was that. It is difficult enough when any relationship breaks up, especially when there is property involved. If to an extent you have existed under the radar it can make it harder. Any hurt you are feeling has to be masked much of the time. You are unlikely to share it with work colleagues. Possibly not with many friends. Nor family. By now my own family were perfectly well appraised of my situation and, in most cases my girlfriends were welcomed into their homes, although I often felt a certain degree of caution. To this day my caution extends to being reluctant to walk down a street hand in hand with my partner of 23 years and wife of 4. In my case there were a handful of good friends who helped me through these situations. People who had similar experiences or just those in whom I'd placed my trust.

> "… as soon as we get into Zone Three (on the Underground), we won't hold hands any more. That's so instinctive it doesn't even get thought about any more, so you will see gay couples assessing a situation meticulously and behaving differently based on the safety of the environment. Which is why when people say it's fine now – it's not, because we're all still editing ourselves." – Ruth Hunt, former CEO of Stonewall

The devilish and delectable singer I have just spoken of was one of those confidantes for me. She continued to entertain even from her bedside when she became ill, amusing me with tales of how she had seen her body float out of the window the previous evening. She seemed to have rather enjoyed that notion and I like to think that when she did slip from our grasp, she did so in full flight wafting her cape behind her.

I will stop for a moment and say that I wish in writing this that I could gather together all the wonderful women I have had the honour of meeting through work. To enjoy again the laughter, the naughty talk, the scrapes, heartaches, headaches and happiness they brought me. To revel in their feistiness and the beauty of their souls. I wish especially this could be the case with my accomplice in life at that big, green store on the corner in Knightsbridge. If she were still here, she would have undoubtedly helped me work out how to resolve some of the challenges I have had in my life. I would have loved to share with her the fact that eventually I got round to using my voice. I say this humbly, in a similar way to her. She died in November 1989, by which time I had escaped from Harrods and was back in a health club environment.

STCC

My next stop was a large tennis and country club, where I had taken up the post of fitness (and unwittingly front of house) manager. There were two spacious, state-of-the-art gyms and a dance studio, all within my remit to schedule, staff and run. I also had duty management responsibilities every Friday night and Saturday. It was a wonderful place to be for someone who had practically been brought up on tennis courts, equipped as it was with over a dozen all-weather outdoor courts, twenty-one covered indoor ones, as well as two pools, a café/bar facility and a snooker hall.

It was a suitably nutty setup in which I had the best of times and the worst of times. Full of madcap tennis coaches and patrons, shenanigans off and on the courts, in the swimming pools and snooker hall, working 6 days a week, running social events on top of my official job functions. It was a place of work that I delighted in going to each day. Until the big takeover. From being a privately run club, it was taken over by a bigger company with bigger fish to fry. And fry away they did.

Most of the directors and people who had employed me had gone. The inevitable day came when one by one they called every senior member of staff into the closed quarters of the general manager's office. The tension in the air was palpable. There was a sickened feeling in all our stomachs. Each returned with their own story and destiny etched on their faces including my partner at work and home, who as tennis manager was very much the heart of the club. My turn came. I was spared the sword. In fact, I was to not only keep my job but gain the additional responsibility of overseeing the reconstruction and refurbishment of a new fitness wing. I was studying for a diploma in management at the time. I guess my face fitted and I had made the right noises. Mixed emotions were prevalent though, personal relief and a sense of excitement tinged with sadness to see so many good friends and colleagues literally depart there and then. Suffice to say that there was a vast amount of change that had gone on and was to go on. I was right there in the mix but to an extent it turned out I was a means to an end. My relationship at home had plummeted, which impacted upon our professional lives as my partner, having lost her job as tennis manager remained as a coach for a time.

When the new fitness block was finished at the club, I was summoned to a quiet office with the visiting regional manager. I had been put under increasingly enormous pressure for the tiniest of things. A lightbulb missing in the gym was apparently sufficient grounds to give me a disciplinary. We are all flawed in one way or another. No matter how determined, focused or ambitious I have been at times, many times I have been my own worst enemy, my own stumbling block. Sometimes through a lack of self-belief, sometimes deferring to others too often rather than trusting in my own instincts, getting the balance between being level headed and not, not asking for help often enough, letting my heart rule my head. With all that was going on around me I had taken my eye off the ball but the blow that was dealt me was harsh. Without any hesitation and without anyone else present he told me he wanted me to leave. "What is the alternative?" I stammered through quivering lips. "There is none," he replied. I picked up my belongings, walked away, called my sister to pour out my sorrows and never looked back.

Crest

Having licked my wounds thoroughly for a short while, I became the manager of the Crest Sports and Leisure Club in Kidbrooke, South London. It was the summer of 1995. I was 36.

A few months before, whilst my life was still rather messy, Marg and I had met. At a hen party. That of a cousin of hers. A small event. I spotted her across a room and thought what a kind person she looked. A novice in the world of lesbianism, she was naturally wary. I just knew that I had met one of the loveliest people ever to cross my path. Sleeping arrangements meaning that we had to share a single bed, the next morning she dropped me off a couple of streets away from the home where I was still living with my long-term girlfriend from the tennis club. As usually happens, a wedding follows a hen party, and the day came two months later. Complete with bronchitis and a heavy cold, I cadged a lift with a friend up to Edinburgh for the nuptials. Marg and I had been put on the same table by the bride at the reception. Things went well despite me not actually being able to speak. The next morning everyone gathered for breakfast and made off for our return journeys home. Marg, who had been sharing a room with her brother, was travelling home with him by train. Having clocked that Marg had not slept in her own bed that night, and as the train pulled out of Waverley Station heading for London, her brother said, "So Marg, I think you might have something to tell me!" And so she spilt the beans.

Our relationship developed from afar and slowly until I incurred the wrath of my erstwhile partner, the tennis coach once too many times. I was sent packing one early June evening landing on Marg's doorstep with a bag in hand into which I had bundled what belongings I could before fleeing the flying laundry basket. "I've left home," I proclaimed. "Can I stay with you tonight?" I looked imploringly into her kind but rightly concerned face and stayed there for several months during which time the nature and strength of our relationship developed.

Crest was the only members club in the portfolio of Circa Leisure who were a leisure centre management company. I was appointed chiefly because my background was solely in the private club world. But this was not the prestigious world of South Kensington, Knightsbridge or the leafy suburbs of Surrey. It was South East London opposite a rather notorious housing estate. It appealed to the part of me who liked adventure, a bit of derring-do, the unconventional. I absolutely loved it!

Still retaining a formality, and what I considered to be a degree of professionalism, by not abbreviating my name, at that time in a work environment I was known as Judith. When the time came for me to leave and I was rejoined at my new place of work by various members from my Crest team one of them who had been a young and shy recreation assistant opened up to me. "You've changed, Boss. I like how you've become more open. I wish you had been more open and socialised with us back at Crest. You were quite distant." Sometimes the people you least expect can teach you a lesson. He was right. My determination to maintain a rigid, professional persona, was a way I thought would gain me respect. I naively also thought that it was necessary in order to hide certain sides of my life and personality but neither were things they had wanted. It is hard to be a mate and a boss to people but in future I always tried my best to adopt that combination and try and strike a delicate balance between the two. He and I still keep in touch and continue to share our mutual respect on social media. He still refers to me as "boss" which both amuses me and fills me with a certain sense of pride.

I was dogged in setting high expectations for myself, the bar so high. And maybe it wasn't necessary to do that. Maybe I should have given myself more slack, relaxed my cover more. Sometimes we try too hard and others' perceptions of us become skewed.

One story I like to share is about one summer evening when I was duty manager at Crest. All dressed up in my designer cream suit, I bent down to pick up some cups from a table and on rising, forgot I was underneath a staircase overhang. It was soon pointed out to me that my suit was being spoiled by the amount of blood pouring on to it. A towel was wrapped around my head and one of the staff members then drove me to Lewisham Hospital A&E. She remained whilst I was taken into a cubicle and then excused herself to resume her shift at the club. She returned after an hour, walked into the same cubicle to see me lying face down on the bed with a sheet over my head. There was a noticeable intake of breath, before she realised that I hadn't actually died in her absence but was actually just being prepped for stitches.

Eventually the decision was made to sell Crest and offload Circa's management of it, also ending my contract. All very straightforward. No hard feelings.

LA Fitness

A new opportunity was just around the corner and one that would leave perhaps the most long-lasting mark on my professional career in the fitness industry.

A new health and fitness company, LA Fitness, had been set up by two men I had worked for at STCC. They had six clubs across London and were set to expand. Having left Crest, and with LA Fitness having acquired an old gym in Bromley, the operations director (and friend) asked me if I would like to go in to manage it. I don't remember deliberating about this. I knew that it would be a good move and fun to work with them again.

And so, I found myself driving everyday to East Street in Bromley, to a dilapidated building that really wasn't safe and that in today's health and safety conscious world would not have been allowed. I quickly put my team together, including a few who moved from Crest to be with me. Even as the building underwent renovations and dust was falling around our ears, aerobics classes still went on in true Brits in the Blitz style. A mixed bag of people put together and relishing each other's company. Working for each other. Playing together. Men and women in the team donning pink tutus, wands in hand as we proudly took part in the first LA Sports Day at Market Sports, Spitalfields, with their goalkeeping Bromley boss performing a backflip to save a goal on the hard tarmac in the 7-a-side football tournament. One of my proudest moments in sport.

From Bromley, I was elevated into the role of sidekick to my friend the operations director, and then into that of regional manager for the south London area. A real family had formed throughout the whole company especially in the early years. We weathered any storms thrown our way, helped each other in our work and partied like you've never seen before, bonded by shared humour and values.

LA was expanding at an almost alarming rate and within 3 years of being there, it was decided to float on the stock market. I was invited to head up an HR department, which I gladly accepted. People management was where my natural skills lay and something I was passionate about. Whilst I wanted to support the company in trying to put suitable and appropriate policies and procedures in place, I also wanted to try to ensure that staff were treated well and given the necessary levels of support they deserved. I was to also gain a diploma in HR.

In those early HR days, I was housed on my own in a small office. Then I got to share it with two male colleagues who would become firm and long-standing friends. Space was tight. Back to back with my training manager I checked in with him, "Are you ready for our meeting?" Swivelling my chair around and clashing knees with him as I did so, he replied, "I'm ready," as both of us let out wry laughs, the third member of that office chuckling quietly in the background.

It would probably be fair to say that the culture of the company, led by the most charismatic and driven of CEOs, was not going to make it easy for progressive HR practices. But over a 5-year period I was able to grow my department from just me to a team of twenty-five. We rolled out my LA Way strategy and staff training programme, but still it was very much an uphill climb with a figurehead who just didn't buy into HR. Creating solid foundations by investment in your staff wasn't given the weight that, in my opinion, it required. The focus was on securing sales and profits. Censure for supposed transgressions, like not meeting your sales figures, was often very tough as I knew first hand as a regional manager. I had stuck it out and got my rewards when I moved into HR and our CEO did have the good grace to acknowledge this. "I gave you a hard time and I really admire you for putting up with it. Now you are the guardian of the company," our CEO told me. That may have been the case but at times it wasn't easy guarding a growing company with a staff of 1,200 and a need to grow profits.

After 5 years of relentlessly pursuing respect for the good HR practices I put in place, and with Marg and I deciding to move out of London to Kent, it felt like the moment to make some big changes in my life. Typically, my decision to leave coincided with our CEO finally holding his hands up to the fact that good HR practices are key to a company's success. He tried to persuade me to stay and promised huge investment in making sure that my strategy was not only implemented but successful. After a long discussion about my intentions he said, "Go away old girl and think about it over the weekend." I had already thought about it, a lot, but confirmed my plans on the Monday afterwards. I was able to map out my departure over a 3-month period including helping to restructure and recruit my successor.

I have kept my reflections about my time at LA Fitness quite short. Eight years is quite a long time. When I joined we had six clubs. When I left, we had 82. We had grown at a furious rate and had become one of the leading health club chains in the country. It was a momentous time. I gained so much experience and quickly. I gained so many friends and quickly. Likeminded people dedicated to hard work and having fun. People and times who will for ever hold a special place in my heart and to every one, I will always be grateful.

I had had many jobs during my career. There were also plenty of interviews I went to and jobs I didn't get. But the time was now ripe for some big changes.

And Beyond

So, what became of this woman who had striven for 21 years in the fitness industry? On moving to Kent, she undertook the renovation and refurbishment of the early 18th-century rural home that she and Marg had found there tucked away into a hill overlooking the glorious orchards and hop fields of the Garden of England. In hindsight taking on so much that was new so soon after leaving a long career and a city that had been home for 25 years was perhaps a big jump. Added to which she had embarked upon a diploma in interior design. A passion since childhood it was now thought timely for her to pursue that professionally. The course was shelved whilst the year-long build went on but after studying for 3 years, finally in November 2008, she qualified. Qualifications were something she hadn't ever found easy. She had always considered them necessary in order to do anything, but for this she worked harder perhaps than for anything before. There really was a lot of sweat and tears. She had set her sights on achieving nothing less than an A grade but had to be satisfied with a B+. Still something to be proud of, but disappointing to have not made her goal. She then set out to market herself as a freelance designer. Smack at the start of a hard recession. In a location she wasn't familiar with. She got a few small projects and delivered some workshops. And started providing high-end B&B in what was now a fully renovated country home complete with contemporary, Indian-styled guest room adding private, fine dining to the offer. Very much a weekend business, with only one room and no room to scale up, it wasn't a business to make a living from. But it was relished and offered a huge sense of fulfilment. And so it was until she became ill and received an M.E. diagnosis in November 2011. Not fully appreciating what this would mean, she naively tried to keep the B&B going until it was impossible. Even making a bed was physically exhausting and dealing with customers, stressful and overwhelming.

So that was my reality. M.E. stopped me from pursuing and building my interior design business. But the reality also was that it had been very hard to get business. It was the recession. I did a lot of marketing but could I have done more? If illness hadn't stepped in, how long would I have given myself to get the business off the ground, start to break even, maybe even make some money? I have felt a lot of guilt leaving the good job I had in London and then not making the next step work out. It is hard work being self-employed, setting up a business on your own. I would have pulled up short and gone back to more regular employment had my health not intervened.

Illness, in a strange way, gave me permission not to feel so guilty anymore. The reality is that now, 8 years later I still wouldn't be able to sustain a regular job. I do worry about what other people think and know that writing, which is what I've spent a lot of my time doing in recent years, isn't perceived by many people to be work. But then in many ways, with everything I've done since leaving London, I have felt a little like an imposter, like I'm playing at whatever it is. As long as the people that matter most, in this case Marg and I, are happy with the way we manage our lives then that should be all that matters. It is no one else's business and logically I know that. People make their lives work in many ways. And as long as there is no negative impact on others, then that should be all that counts.

I am not going to talk about my music and singing here because, despite many other people insisting on referring to those as a career, especially once I had brought out my first album, I have never seen it like that. I am not a professional musician. I have never earned any form of living from music. I have never really earned anything from it. We have spent a lot on it. Someone once said that they had to choose between making a new album or putting central heating in. Making good music is a costly affair and not always appreciated by the broader public.

But as far as a career goes, it depends of course how you regard the word career. I prefer to regard how I spend my time now as a vocation. I guess for me, and I would argue for a lot of people, career means something that earns you a living rather than simply a calling. The Google definition of career goes as follows: "An occupation undertaken for a significant period of one's life and with opportunities for progress." In that respect, therefore, I suppose I am wrong.

So who am I now? What do I do? Does it even matter? Do we have to label ourselves? When filling out embarkation cards at Marrakesh airport returning from our holiday in Morocco in December, 2018, Marg asked me, "What are you putting as your occupation this time?", "I think I'll be singer songwriter", I replied. We both saw the funny side of her question, but it did have a deeper meaning for me.

In the last 14 years since I ceased to be employed, I have written interior designer, B&B proprietor and musician. I guess I could start putting writer, or retired, but I'm not.

Writing in some shape or form, performing occasionally, is what I do now. And I really hope that I can make more progress and have some measure of success through this way of life, whether artistic recognition, some financial reward, plain enjoyment or all of the above. That I can continue to learn. That I can share my music and my books with others if they are happy to join in.

And so, to close this piece I return to gyms and the fitness industry.

I left that behind as a career a long time ago. I am retaining links to it by trying where possible to use leisure centres and gyms to exercise once again in a formal setting.

And we are keeping it in the family. Marg, having left the worlds of social housing, international cultural relations and the fight against global poverty behind, is now the CEO of a health and leisure company. In addition, we sit down each year for 5 minutes to hold an AGM for the Little Funky Fitness Company. I still own the domain name and company name for a dormant company. Back when we moved to Kent, I was keen to join a quality health club and was dismayed to have to travel quite far afield to find one. So, I set about planning my own. I had a site searcher. I got a gang of ex-LA Fitness staff together to pool their expertise. I came close. I had the vision, but it wasn't to be.

Perhaps by not giving up that company name, I hold onto a glimmer of hope that maybe, just maybe one day, I may be able to turn that vision into a reality. Or I may decide to finally give in and give it up before the next AGM comes around.

For now, I am content with pursuing my new ambitions. I have goals. I have ticked one or two off my list. And I will keep adding more. I made my start and I am not going to stop now.

Travel

California Dreaming

I have been fortunate to travel to the USA several times. To Miami and New York with Marg and for work purposes to Dallas, Texas, Phoenix, Arizona and San Diego, in California. I spent 2 months in California straight after finishing college staying in the desert near downtown 29 Palms and visiting Yosemite, Lake Tahoe, Palm Springs, Las Vegas and Los Angeles for the first time. One day whilst in LA, I was out swimming and got sucked into a riptide. I found myself fighting hard to get out. Imagine drainage tunnels with water swirling and rushing along with immense force, turning you around and around like the contents of a washing machine. Eventually a break appears and you are thrown out of it, tumbling on to the shore, a half mile from where you started. Gasping for breath, shaken and stirred, I emerged totally unlike Ursula Andress or Halle Berry. Relieved, I staggered back to where I had left the others a way up the beach.

Years later, Marg and I would travel to California. Having previously been at odds, me preferring to have knowledge of where we would be staying, Marg preferring the more freeform approach, we booked accommodation for only the first few days in San Fransisco, the only other advance booking made being to hire a convertible. That car was our first experience of top down, wind blowing in our hair, sunshine on our heads, shades on, girls on a mission. It was an exhilarating 3-week trip down Highway 1 into Mexico and back up to Los Angeles to stay in the Hollywood Hills with family before flying home. Whilst there, we were on the guest list at The Roxy on Sunset Strip for a Rufus Wainwright concert in the days before he was well known. Marg later met him properly when he was better known and she was on the guest list at a reception for the actual queen. We decided each day where we would stay the next. "Shall we head for Santa Barbara tomorrow and maybe stay two nights there?" Suggested Marg. "Sounds like a plan, honey," I replied as I lay back in my seat, stuck my bare feet on the dash, tipped my baseball cap back and said "Step on the gas, baby!" My smile building, a chuckle letting rip as Marg stepped on the accelerator. "I love road trips with you," she said. And off we went feeling greatly amused, a warmth throughout our bodies and delighting in the whole experience and each other's company. I read recently that, "the best road trips have few set plans. They're about the thrill of discovery, of not knowing what comes next." This trip was testament to that sentiment.

We spent time in San Diego where we ate the largest and most succulent of oysters. Next came Santa Barbara, Carmel and Monterey where we went to see the then new film *Titanic* and over indulged in an extraordinary fashion at a seafood restaurant in Monterey Bay. We blamed this on the delayed food service and having wine poured into our glasses really quite unknowingly. Whilst staying in Monterey, we read John Steinbeck's *Cannery Row* to each other at night – the book being set there.

"Cannery Row's inhabitants are, as the man once said, 'whores, pimps, gamblers, and sons of bitches,' by which he meant everybody. Had the man looked through another peephole he might have said, 'saints and angels and martyrs and holy men,' and he would have meant the same thing.", Marg read. Which of the those best suited us I dare not say. A thought-provoking book it captured our imagination as we wondered around the streets and shores making our way around that place and through the book.

"It has always seemed strange to me. The things we admire in men, kindness and generosity, openness, honesty, understanding and feeling, are the concomitants of failure in our system. And those traits we detest, sharpness, greed, acquisitiveness, meanness, egotism and self-interest, are the traits of success. And while men admire the quality of the first they love the produce of the second." As I read this out loud it became a point of discussion. "Which of those qualities do you believe contributes to being a successful person?", Marg asked. "I would like to think openness, honesty and understanding do," I replied, knowing that it was perhaps a vain hope. Such observations floated around in our heads as we continued our journey.

We sped along Big Sur, stopping sometimes to take in the spectacular views, Marg striding out onto vertiginous rocky outcrops whilst I grimaced further back and held my breath. We stayed in a log cabin in the redwood forests, still possibly the best night's sleep I have ever had; the trees creating a canopy to protect us, towering overhead and climbing high into the stratosphere. Cosying up in front of the fire, books and glasses of wine in hand, with only the murmur of the breeze blowing through and the sound of wildlife scuttling over our roof for company. Indulging my love of small, quirky places. We spent time in small towns, staying in basic motels whilst enjoying the local delights of junior baseball league games munching on pretzels, and burgers, getting underneath the real life of the communities. We stayed at a spa with health giving but odious smelling sulphur tubs, and in one city had to vacate our lodgings very late at night when we realised it was predominantly a gay men's meeting place and the comings and goings would as likely keep us awake for hours. We were free and easy. Without question in our top five holidays and one to be repeated.

A Handful of Passions

Design

A friend of mine once noted that when I see good interior design or architecture or styles that I like my arms flap. I get very excited. Uplifted. Animated. Inspired.

They are things that get my juices flowing. I love reading about other people's design interests. Culture. Creativity. I love going into rooms and buildings that are stylish, innovative. Where care has been taken and attention to detail paid. I can just sit in such a room and find myself transported. Motivated. The world becomes full of possibilities.

> "Perhaps believing in good design is like believing in God,
> it makes you an optimist."
> – *Sir Terence Conran*

My environment affects my mood, my wellbeing. Whether it is where I shop, where I sleep, where I work, where I eat. Where I meet friends, where I spend my time, where I breathe. Where I watch, look and listen.

Happiness is the Victoria and Albert Museum. Craven Cottage Football Ground. The Mondrian Hotel on the Southbank. The Citizen M Hotel in Rotterdam. Shepherds huts, cool campervans. Homes I've lived in. The pages of *Elle Decoration*. Terence Conran. Modernist houses. Shabby chic – within reason. Industrial buildings. Less is more.

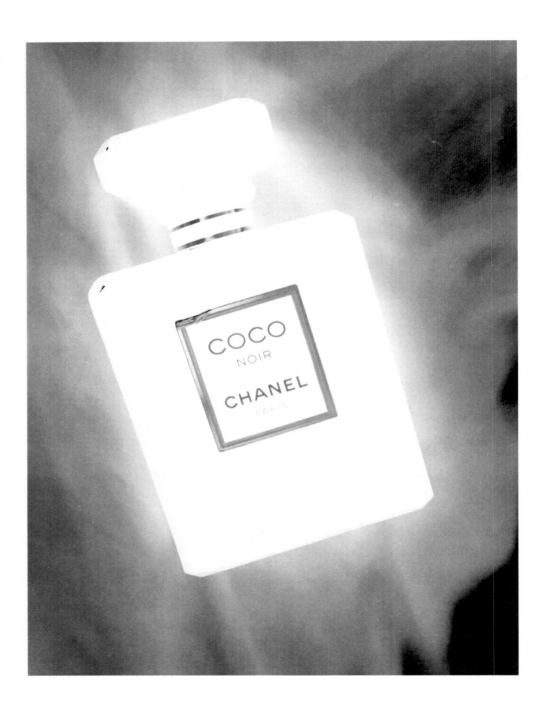

Chanel

"Keep your heels, head and standards high."
– Coco Chanel

I don't wear high heels. Not real high heels. Ever.

I try to remember to hold my head up high. Sometimes it droops.

I always try to maintain the very highest of standards. Sometimes those may slip. More often I set them so high that I find them hard to reach and maintain.

She proffered up an unmatchable simplicity and sophistication in her clothing and perfumes. She was a pioneer.

I wear Chanel perfume. Coco. Coco Noir. I sometimes wear Coco body lotion. When I want to feel really special, am away from home or just need a big lift I use Coco shower gel.

I have been known when attending music festivals where bathroom facilities are few, to adorn myself with leopard skin swimsuit, sarong and ... Chanel.

I love Chanel.

Cats – a story of two tails

January 2014.

The dead of night.

A time of very poor health for me.

I had developed a habit of getting up and sitting quietly in the kitchen, often on a rug in the middle of the floor. I felt like a raft, adrift at sea, encircled by fish.

The fish was Bertie. A cat. One that had become a complete recluse following the demise of his brother, Earl, 6 weeks before. We had barely seen him during that time but then he had started a nightly wander into the kitchen where he found me contemplating and reflecting, with only the moonlight and stars providing light.

It was calm. A peaceful, a non-threatening environment. If I spoke to him, I did it gently, trying to coax some communication from him. To comfort him. He would circle the rug working out what was seated on it. Safe, as long as he didn't touch it. In a way, we were both rafts at sea. Having done this for a few nights, he then became rather adventurous and crept onto the rug to join me. Let's not get too close though. And then a few days later when Marg and I were sitting on the sofa in the kitchen, he strolled in as bold as you like, positively pounced onto our laps and never looked back.

Earl and Bertie. Brixton brothers found on a building site, they lived their first 2 years in Blackheath housed by the Celia Hammond Trust. And then one spring bank holiday in 1997, we went to collect them. Two 2-year old black and white cats. Frightened little creatures, we secured them very much against their wishes in baskets on the back seat of the car and took them back home again to Brixton.

Earl settled in nicely, showing signs of being in charge and comfortable in company. But Bertie was a terrified little animal. For weeks he would cower in corners, flee to the top of doors on the highest floors of the house and sneak into unused chimney flues. He gingerly crept out for food, but remained hidden when people were around. Even us. They both seemed especially frightened of men. We wondered what had befallen them on that building site. They were such dear little animals. Whatever had happened to them we would make sure they were well looked after and protected by us.

In the summer of 2004, we upped sticks and moved to Kent. Once again, the boys were safe in their despised baskets on the back seat of Marg's car. Earl had been housed overnight at the local vet to ensure his security. We had to borrow a cat-sized rat trap to try and catch Bertie. He was smart, knew that strange goings on were afoot, the status quo shaken and evaded us at every turn. When the morning came for the move, Marg popped round to the corner shop (the last time for many years that we would be able to say that) and I remained at home pottering around in our bedroom with the rat trap for company – Bertie boy nowhere to be seen. And then he strolled in. I swiftly closed the door behind him and somehow ushered him into the trap. We later extracted him and hustled him into his basket, his heart-breaking cries unabating despite our attempts to speak soothingly to him.

And so, the four of us arrived in the Kent countryside.

It's fair to say that they probably adjusted to this enormous change more easily than us, certainly better than I.

We had been advised to lock the cats into one room for a few days. The first night we set them up in their en suite room next to ours and went to bed. In the morning, we woke up and sat looking out at our new and magnificent views. Then we heard the patter of tiny paws.

Country cats they became within 24 hours. They were born to this lifestyle and were deliriously happy, although Bertie remained very timid. They even withstood the 10-month renovation and refurbishment of the house, secreting themselves in the garden or the farthest reaches of any part of the building that remained untouched when the workmen were present. When we asked for a cat flap tunnel to be built into the significantly thick walls of our new kitchen the builders were somewhat bemused. They hadn't realised we had cats.

After living their idyllic country life for 9 years, Earl became very poorly, and we had to make the painful decision to have him put to sleep. This was done at home. We had a large pit dug in our back garden and buried him in a box wrapped in a cosy blanket with a poem that I had written about him. It was a moving ceremony. We planted a rosemary bush on top of him in honour of the fact that underneath a rosemary bush was his favourite place to snooze.

Following our time at sea and on sofas together, Bertie gradually became the friendliest, most sociable animal you could imagine. No longer frightened of anyone, he would invite strokes and cuddles from all and sundry. He became my truest of friends. There at my side throughout my illness. Chatting. Snuggling in. Doing the potty things that cats do. Lying on my head at night. Waking us up at some horribly early time in the morning. Doing yoga with me. Bouncing around in the garden even until a few days before he too had to leave us.

He was 22 in June 2017 and very suddenly started to lose his appetite and the use of his vital organs. Still sprightly and fit looking, he was the most adorable and remarkable of animals. I miss him still. We have a shrine of sorts to him on a windowsill with a fabulous canvas photograph of him keeping an eye on us as we pottered in the garden just a few days before he died. His ashes are still kept in a rather fetching cardboard can.

Sometime soon we will replace them both but for now they live, and will remain so fondly etched, in our memories.

Copens

There are sections in the broadsheets in which public figures are asked various questions about themselves. One of the questions is along the lines of, "Apart from property, what is the most expensive thing you have ever bought?"

My answer to that would be a car. Not even a particularly expensive car, but a new car. The only brand-new car that either Marg or I have ever bought. Because I am not massively materialistic and have never actually had the funds to invest in something fresh off the production line, I had never entertained the idea of owning something of such standing. Sure, I had dreamt that one day I'd own a jeep –the mucky old type you would have seen in M*A*S*H. And an Aston Martin, early James Bond style. But for most of us, those things are dreams.

But then, there was that lazy Sunday morning in the spring of 2004. Marg and I were lounging in bed perusing the papers and, as I was leafing through the *Sunday Times Magazine*, I paused. There before me was an advertisement for the cutest little car I had ever set eyes on. It looked a little like Noddy's car, although I doubted whether Big Ears would have fitted inside. I read the details: a two-seater convertible with an electronic roof that folded into the boot, heated leather seats and a 750cc engine, which for the uninitiated is no more than a motorbike engine, although I hasten to add, with turbo.

"I have to have one of those!", I proclaimed to Marg, who made suitably soothing noises. The thing is, I really did have to have one. Very rarely do I set my cap at something seemingly so extravagant. More common is that I can be doggedly clear whether I like something or not. But that doesn't mean I expect to get it.

Second hand was not an option for this new model. They were yet to roll off the production line. But luckily there was a dealership not far from us. After a brief cooling off period to consider this potential purchase, 4 weeks later we took possession of a shiny, new, silver Daihatsu Copen. Red leather upholstery and trim. We sailed out of there and into an 11-year relationship that was to be one of the best in my life. That car was my pride and joy. It started life in south London and went with us to our new life in east Kent a few months later.

Everywhere I took it, whether along sleepy country lanes and seaside towns, or the clogged-up streets of the capital, people would take a second look, smile, wave or give me a thumbs up as I bopped along, top down at any given opportunity. It weathered brutish four-wheel drives trying to lord it over me on tight country bends. It handled rough terrains with dignity. It sailed past more powerful beasts with flare and graced many a driveway and roadside parking spot. It even caught the eye of a young and dare I suggest, rather cocksure member of the Kent constabulary. I had genuinely overlooked a rather large roadside sign and whipped the wheel leftwards to take an innocent short cut home. A few short yards into the lane a uniformed gentleman flagged me down.

"Did you not see the sign stating that this road is only for access, Madam?"

"No officer I didn't."

"Perhaps you should get your eyes tested Madam?"

"As it happens, I have an appointment tomorrow."

I wasn't trying to be facetious, even if he was. It just slipped out. And it was true. I did have an eye test the following day. But I think he was eager to claim a scalp and slapped a caution on me. My Copen and I had been well and truly copped.

Yes, my little beeper bewitched me and many others, until the day came, in the summer of 2015, that we had to part company. The car went to a man who had such a love of Copens that not only had he travelled down from Leeds to collect it, but would be using it for parts for a sort of Copen organ donation scheme. Somewhere up north parts of my little beeper are coasting around giving delight to someone. LVO4FON I adored you. Thank you.

For 3 barren years I contented myself with driving our second-hand Mini Countryman, and an old and sluggish Peugeot handed down to me by my Dad. When the Peugeot's time was up, we searched online for second-hand Copens, enlisting a trusted friend who found us a bright red 2008 edition on sale near Manchester. I took off up north to stay with another friend and found myself somewhere deep in the Cheshire countryside doing a test drive, quickly being reminded how in touch with the vehicle you really are in a car like that. Every bump and grind is experienced and shudders through your body. Not a high-performance car, not a smooth ride, but a total joy.

The deal being done, my Mancunian based friend and I went out to celebrate. Then, having made our best attempt at being ladies that lunch amongst the tanned, groomed and good of Wilmslow, the little red beeper and I set off home to Kent. When I got home, I realised I'd driven a long way in something not much more robust than a 10-year-old dinky toy, but I had a beam across my face as wide as the ocean. I had been reunited with something that had given me so much pleasure. Almost a part of me. Simple. Stylish. Sassy. A real little smasher.

Football

When I was young, I wasn't allowed to play football at school, or in any other official capacity. It was the 1960s. It wasn't a girls' sport. I could end this piece there because for me it says so much.

Girls played hockey. A far more dangerous sport. Why was it considered more appropriate than football? Was it considered at all? I'm sure there have been studies conducted into this matter, but I am content to state that they would be bunkum.

Fortunately, my family never considered football inappropriate and I played it. A lot. Not in any organised fashion or team, but with two male cousins on patches of land near our homes. We were a tribe although we supported different teams. And we imagined ourselves to be members of those teams. We took turns in goal. Dribbled. Shot. Scored. Didn't score. Tackled. Headed. Got bruises. Got scrapes. I was tiny. Tich they called me. I'm sure I came off quite badly. But I had a blast. Together, late on a Saturday night, we would sit and watch *Match of the Day*, eating sandwiches of crusty bread filled with real butter, mounds of ham, spoonful's of mustard and all washed down with steaming milky coffees. We shared football magazines: *Goal* and *Shoot*. We traded football cards from the fag packets of our parents or a random cereal packet. I had the Subbuteo. I kept scrapbooks. Occasionally we would get taken to a real match. Stoke City v Manchester United being one I recall reasonably clearly. Or Derby County where I would be out at the front of the terraces with a stool to stand on so that I could see over the barrier.

Man Utd were my team. Posters plastered my walls along with Donny and Elvis. I wrote off for autographs and got some very good ones back in return. I'm not sure that would happen now. Georgie Best was the man of the moment. There was even a record about him, "Belfast Boy", which was an early purchase in my record collecting history. I was a member of his fan club. I vaguely remember being able to go and see his clothes shop on a rare trip to Manchester. Or am I imagining that? Maybe I only dreamt it. Best was beautiful, an enigma and a pure genius on the football field.

My footballing prowess, and all those hours weaving around on those bits of garden and grass, came in handy eventually and unexpectedly. I beavered away at school hoping to become a good hockey player. I was neither a natural defender nor attacker. We got swapped in and out of positions and then one summer evening, I was asked to be a stand-in goalkeeper. "You've really found your niche," said the umpire and part-time coach, who was also the mother of one of my friends. And I had. I was 16 and within weeks playing for the town.

My first match was a rain-drenched affair that we lost 14–0. You may have expected that would have been my last. But it wasn't. I was picked for the county under 21 team not long afterwards. People say you have to be crazy to play in goal. I would agree. In those days, the only protection you had were kickers and pads – the latter I dutifully cleaned more than once a week with canvas tennis shoe whitener, the former I polished until they shone. We had no chest or face guards. The one time I did wear face protection was in Germany during a county

tournament one hot and sweaty week in May 1978. So hot and sweaty, in fact, that my face guard kept slipping and, since it was obscuring my view, I cast it aside. We would play mixed matches at school and more than once a ball would come flying at me, hit with some force by a grammar school boy, missing my ribs by millimetres. I played in goal like a footballer: taking out forwards as they pursued the ball with swift sliding tackles to ensure the ball was swept out of harm's way just occasionally taking their sticks with it, belting goal kicks with the might of a well-practiced right foot. And my own stick would be employed with the all the technique learnt in many years of tennis coaching. I relied totally on instinct and my reflexes rather than size to protect myself and my goalmouth.

This continued into my college days until all that diving around, using my left knee as a hinge to propel me up and down, backwards and forward whilst my right performed its role, took its toll. The knee had given up. Heavily strapped, heavily swollen after each match, I had taken it as far as it would go. And so, my final match arrived. Borough Road Ladies – having already come top of our league – arrived at Chiswick Sports Ground one Saturday for the grand finale of the 1980/81 season. It was sort of our FA Cup Final. I don't remember who we played but it went to penalties. England versus Germany this wasn't, but we were victorious. And I saved the crucial flick. I was hoisted onto my team mates' shoulders and carried off. And with that I hung up my kickers and pads. I was never to play hockey again. I was 22.

My love for football waned then until, along with a partner in my early 30s, I would travel – sometimes in the space of one night – from south London and back up to Leeds to watch her beloved team. "We are so proud, we shout it out loud, we love you Leeds, Leeds, Leeds," rang around inside the ground and following a win, in the car on the long journey home. The best chip butties I have ever eaten were from a shop outside Elland Road Football Ground. Her passion I admit, was off the scale and any that I had had paled into insignificance. She vented any fire and passion in her belly at those matches and when watching her team on TV. It was almost frightening to behold but admirable too. The fury and fanaticism that football inspires in people will always fascinate me.

Into my late 30s, I announced to Marg that I would like to follow a football team. I was denying myself what was part of my very being. "I've settled on the criteria. They have to be accessible location and cost wise, so a lower league team is okay. They have to be managed by someone credible. The ground needs to appeal. They need to have a strip we like." All of these things matter in life. Style and substance.

Fulham it was to be. When they were in the Second Division. We started going along to matches and even got a couple of friends involved. And then we all bought season tickets for the cute and characterful Craven Cottage. They did well. They even made it to the Europa League Cup Final one season. They never had a lot of money spent on them and always seemed to be full of academy players or those playing in their twilight years, but that was part of their charm. As was the ground. Wooden seats to this day in the Johnny Haynes Stand where we sat in the same seats game after game and mine, when they talked of plans to develop the ground and sell off those seats, I secured the purchase of. There were mixed feelings when those expansion plans got shelved. I was never to bring that seat home but did get to sit in it a few more times on the banks of Thames next to Putney Bridge. I wonder how many more backsides have graced it in the years since – getting up, sitting down, sticking their empty drinks bottles and hot dog wrappers underneath it as they watch the fortunes of our team ebb and flow. You can take all the big, glossy clubs and I do enjoy watching them, but the smaller clubs have so much to offer and give you such a sense of accessibility and reality.

Moving to Kent meant we gave up our season tickets. I have only managed to get to one or two matches a season since then. I maintained my membership, wanting to remain associated with my tribe as a card-carrying member of FFC. One of those rare matches that I did get to was against Liverpool in the February of the 2012/13 season. Fulham were doing very badly, as they are now, and I am reminded of a quote from the film *The Bromley Boys*: "It is easy to follow success." A sentiment I relate to. At that stage, they seemed to be heading for relegation, but they had beaten Man Utd 2 days before and that night, drew magnificently with Liverpool providing fans with a spectacle of a game as well as hope and optimism. We were turning a corner. Things were looking up. And then the next day they sacked the manager. His name was René Meulensteen, and I later read an interview with him in which he said that afterwards he had been wandering down the King's Road trying to make sense of his circumstances and "was struggling with confusion in broad daylight". A few years later, I fed that line into a song, "That's What the Whisky's For". I thought it very poignant. Beautiful words for a sometimes brutal, always fickle, but beautiful game.

"To Judy from Mr Warren on leaving Shobnall Primary School, 1970"

When you're old and by the fire,
And you think of days gone by,
You'll remember school at Shobnall
With a teardrop in your eye.
You'll recall each treasured memory,
In the scrapbook of your mind,
And you'll wish you could recapture
All those days you left behind.
Then you'll whisper in the darkness,
As you take your evening rest,
"I remember Mr Warren—
But who was Georgie Best!"

History and Heritage

I devour books about the historical endeavours of people such as Scott and Shackleton. The same goes for musical archives showing the *Old Grey Whistle Test, Top of the Pops* – the singers and musicians I admire. I love footage of sporting achievements such as the first 4-minute mile, the Berlin Olympic Games, England winning the World Cup, Virginia Wade and Andy Murray winning Wimbledon. I am drawn to the stories behind them. War too, the 2 World Wars, the Vietnam War. I can watch documentaries and films about these for hours. One I watched recently was about the Assad Dynasty in Syria. I couldn't help likening that smiling face of Bashar Al-Assad and his tightly clipped moustache to another dictator from an earlier time and the destruction they both went on to inflict. What lies behind those eyes, in the minds of such men? What is it about them and those wars that bewitch us? Many of us have personal connections through relatives who took part, photographs and memorabilia passed down through our families that make these things resonate more personally.

As I write, we are due to commemorate the end of the bloodbath that was the First World War. We will soon be wearing our poppies adopted as a symbol of Remembrance. Peter Jackson has just released a film: *They Shall Not Grow Old*. This revolves around original film footage from the First World War brought to life through colour and sound treatments. We find ourselves right there in the trenches or on those fields strewn with bodies, barbed wire and mud. We see the faces and hear the voices of those men full of hope or despair, torn apart or miraculously evading their apparent destiny.

Four years ago, I found myself immersed in the documentary series *Britain's Great War*. And one evening I was stopped in my tracks. There in a grainy image at the top of a steep bank where hundreds and hundreds of ragged fighting men were gathered and seated on the ground, stood a tall, handsome, elegant officer with a slightly longer clipped moustache, and I recognised him instantly as my grandfather. I launched myself at the TV controls and played it back. Paused it. Took a photograph. Then moved it on and sure enough there he was again, this time on the bridge overlooking the bank. Cigarette in hand, leaning nonchalantly against a wall. Although we were unable to find conclusive evidence that it was him, or what he was doing there, family members have sewn together a patchwork of information allowing us to believe, aside from the striking resemblance, that it was indeed him. It spurred me on to find out why he was there.

The bridge was that of St Quentin. It was taken at the end of September/beginning of October 1918, freed by the North Staffs Regiment. My grandfather who was from Staffordshire, was an officer in the Royal Medical Corps. We have a letter written by him on 16 May 1918 from 26th Field Ambulance BE7 in France. Likely a temporary hospital, it was attached to the 8th Division who took part in the battle of St Quentin.

There is a further suggestion from undated letters that at some stage, he suffered a serious loss of blood and was returned to England on a hospital ship. It materialised that he was not injured but suffering from something rather less dramatic, rather more run of the mill and yet all the same unpleasant. One of many pencil-written letters to my grandmother explains this: "My dear little Dorothy – am afraid am going to be sent down the line sick those things I told you about have been bleeding a fair bit and I can't ride or walk much. It has been an excellent tour thank you and tell Mac I'll bring back a Mills bomb just to show Rose that the weight is over 1lb – of course don't know whether I'll get to England or not. Don't write anymore till you hear again. Yours Bill."

Through those grim, desolate and ravaged war years, he wrote lovingly to my grandmother, copies of just a few included here. Love letters in their truest sense. Written with plain faced aplomb and a resignation to his lot, but with at times a wonderful honesty and sensibility.

"My dear Dorothy. It seems ages since I saw you and I haven't had a single letter from you yet. I left the ambulances 2 days ago and the letters hadn't had time to reach me and heaven knows how long I'll be here so it's no good getting them sent on but I'm longing to hear how you are getting on – there's a train here now but they wait days sometimes before filling up and there's hardly anything doing on the front. Went on the river here yesterday – thought of the Trent – and it's very deserted too. If you write here I suppose they'll send it on ... am getting quite nervous about you. Don't know why. Love Bill."

Ultimately, he served in military hospitals in the north of England, one being the Abram Peel War Hospital in Bradford where the 437 beds were under the command of Captain William Leitrim Clements. It was one of eight hospitals in the country for shell shock victims.

It is hard to imagine just what life was like during that war, and after it, for William Leitrim and all the others who returned carrying a burden of anguish, pain and suffering. Hard to imagine when I look at a photograph of that strikingly handsome young man in his tennis whites, leaning casually against an umpire's chair, before his life was thrown into the unimaginable spin of war. A medical graduate from Durham University. A rowing and athletics blue who had been a gap-year pioneer taking off to South Africa where he is said to have become a Mountie, leading me to presume that whilst there he may have served in the Royal Canadian Mounted Police in the 2nd Boer War. A young man who had got to the last eight of the mixed doubles at Wimbledon just months before The First World War broke out. A man of stature, of enormous character, eccentric with a huge sense of fun and adventure and the looks of a matinee idol. Hard to imagine what lay inside the minds of the people who had experienced such horrors and hardships. How it marked them, their lives, personalities, futures and families through time.

Wake Up Now

(I wrote this in 2014. Originally intended as a song it was inspired by the conflict in Syria.)

We're all trying to make our way with our lives,
Its not a fight for the best position.
Better help each other get on otherwise,
We'll meet in a big collision.

Wake up world, wake up now.
Wake up world, wake up.
Wake up world, wake up-hey
We got to live a better way.

What the hell is going on universe,
Not time for the Armageddon,
Got to stop the wars, put humanity first,
Got to stop the lies we're fed on.

Wake up world, wake up now.
Wake up world, wake up.
Wake up world, wake up-hey
We got to live a better way.

Wake up world, wake up now.
Wake up world, wake up.
Wake up world, wake up now
We got to live a better way.

Where's the heart, soul, hope on this earth,
Have we lost all sense of reason,
Got to end the hate, got to end the hurt,
Bring some peace, bring some freedom.

Wake up world, wake up now.
Wake up world, wake up.
Wake up world, wake up now
We got to live a better way.

The Leitrim and indeed the Clements in my grandfather's name, William Leitrim Clements, is part of an Irish heritage. His father had come from Ireland around 1880 and had built a home in Burton upon Trent called Gortmonley House, after the place where he had been born and raised near Strabane in County Tyrone. The Staffordshire version was the house where my grandfather, mother and I were then raised. My great-grandfather set up a medical practice there where my grandfather and subsequently a few of my uncles joined him.

Growing up, there was an understanding of an Irish connection. Legend had it that we were descendants of the Earl of Leitrim, through an illegitimate line. My grandfather had a gold signet ring with the Leitrim crest on it. When I was a child, a large family group gathered as a working party to clear out the cellar at Gortmonley House, which had by then simply become known as No. 6, St Paul's Square. Amongst the cobwebs, newts and assorted junk and memorabilia accumulated over many years and probably lying unused since the cellar was employed as a bomb shelter during the Second World War, we unearthed a large picture of the same crest.

Various family members had done some research into our ancestry. It is interesting and sometimes important to know where you have come from as well as from whom. Marg and I very voluntarily took up the baton on two trips during the 1990s to investigate further. This being a time before the internet was of much assistance, we embarked on an extraordinary treasure hunt, initially spending a week in Northern Ireland, the land of Marg's own birth, and a couple of years later another in Southern Ireland. We roamed the lanes and dirt tracks by car, and when roads ran out, continued on foot. We came across a family pile, somewhat in need of care and attention, but lived in still by a very distant relative with the rather marvellous name of Headly Vickers Strutt. Sadly, we didn't get to meet him. We stayed in a similarly large but minor stately home with another couple who ran it as a rather shabby chic (not in a trendy way), fabulous guest house. They also wrote books about the many wonderful uses for potatoes. "Come cousin Jude, let's share a glass of wine and discuss our history." Out came documents, books, photographs. It was a very good discussion and a very good glass of wine.

We toured villages, golf courses, graveyards. Had afternoon tea with vicars. Visited tombs in Dublin where the remains of the Leitrim dynasty are embalmed and secured for posterity. Talked to historians in the comfort of hotels and even a very elderly one in Downings, in the wilds of County Donegal next to the now well-known, Rosapenna golf course. He rather precariously climbed on to a small stepladder and pulled out a roll of wallpaper with the Leitrim family tree pencilled in on the back. It was a labour of love, an obsession and a jigsaw puzzle that was edging closer to completion.

Already knowing that one of my grandfather's cousins was known to have said that the Earl of Leitrim was, "an uncle of father's", we secured enough evidence to conclude that we were descended from either the "wicked" 3rd Earl of Leitrim or one of his siblings. There will likely remain one missing piece of our own jigsaw puzzle. We were unable to determine exactly which sibling. It was very common in the 18th and 19th centuries to pass on the family name and other trinkets to illegitimate offspring, even if through the female line. This is why the name Leitrim and Clements and that gold ring has continued, and will doubtless continue, to be passed down through the generations in our family. Always and very conventionally through eldest sons.

People – what is it about them?

These are just a handful of people who have captured my imagination and my heart. Through being an avid reader of biographies, autobiographies, memoir. A devotee of documentaries on the radio and screens of all sizes and time spent engaging with their work and exploits.

Noel Coward. His wit. His words. His songs. His flamboyance. His cigarette holder. His silk dressing gown. I used to listen to his music when I was young. I often thought my dad dressed a little like him. I even wore an old dressing gown a little like his that had belonged to my grandmother.

Marlene Dietrich. Her vampishness. Her sultry hooded eyes. Her smoky voice. Her cigarette holder. Her sometimes androgynous dress sense. Her ability to reinvent herself years before Madonna, Kylie or Lady Gaga. "Falling in Love Again".

Ernest Shackleton. His being a giant amongst men and mankind. His resilience. His determination. His humanity. His leadership skills. His heroism.

Dusty. Her voice. Her vulnerability. Her persona. Her true personality. Her fabness.

The Beatles. Their words. Their music. Their wit. Their style. For being musical pioneers.

Warhol. His Fifteen Minutes of Fame. His art. His ground-breaking style. His fascination with the world quite rightly.

Lee Alexander McQueen. For being a troubled but valiant soul. For the artistry in his couture. For "Savage Beauty".

Banksy. His art. His cheek. His ability to hide. His shredding device.

Georgie Best. Just because.

Don't Know

Don't know

Don't know

Don't know

Don't know

Don't know

Don't Know

Don't know

Don't know

Don't know

Don't know

Don't know

Don't Know

Don't know

Don't know

Don't know

Don't know

Don't know

Don't Know

Don't know

Don't know

Don't know

Don't know

Don't know

Don't Know

Don't know

Don't know

Don't know

Don't know

Don't know

Don't Know

Don't know

Don't know

Prejudice

Initially, I was going to include a whole section on prejudices. But I quickly recognised that what I have to say about prejudice is a passion. And rather than start from scratch and over complicate things, I would return to the notes I wrote to support the writing of "Don't Judge Me No More", a song on my first album. After all, I had probably said what I wanted to say then. So rather than rewrite the script I would simply embellish that, dip my toe into a few more thoughts and flirt with a few little quotations and references to the subject that I have picked up along the way and grown fond of.

"It's an interesting age to be, I think."
– Emma Thompson reflecting on turning 60, in 2019

"I'm always disappointed that women don't celebrate being
60 more than they do." – Mary Beard

I was struck by this conversation on *Front Row*, late in October 2018. Why is it that women who are 60 don't celebrate their age? I would suggest that the answer is because the emphasis in society is very much on youth and fostering the young. This means that older people, generally, are directly and indirectly discriminated against and shy away from celebrating it. Setting out on a new vocation or career at a later stage in life, brings you up against a variety of obstacles often not obvious. The benefits that age and experience can bring are boundless and yet it can be very hard to find work or opportunity regardless of talent. "Beauty of Youth", a song on my second album that accompanies this book, was written with that in mind. "Youth is not a time of life but a state of mind." I would like to take credit for that but alas I can't, although I firmly believe it.

Often discrimination isn't direct, but imposed by society and the supposed norms we feel we are expected to live by. The sadness is quite often that when people don't get something instinctively, they don't try to. Instead they react in a variety of ways that can all and equally be hugely prejudicial, damaging and painful.

When we face prejudice, we also react in a variety of ways. If we actively choose to remain silent and don't protest openly, it doesn't mean that the depth of feeling is any less. I have never been a marcher or a great banner waving protester. Perhaps that was borne out of fear of retribution. Perhaps just because I prefer to speak out quietly. It doesn't become me to get vexed and I would be wary of the consequences for myself and others.

I protected myself and my sexuality by not being overt about it, and considered that my natural way and my right.

Having experienced sexual discrimination and bullying personally, I also experienced it professionally and have been a witness to it in several work environments. I offered my own answer and tried to instigate change by becoming an HR professional.

If people don't understand the way someone else is, or lives their life, then they should at the very least manage that in an intelligent, civilised and respectful way. This is the very least we should all be able to expect from each other. "Don't Judge Me No More" was triggered by two instances where I was spoken to with a lack of respect and consideration. This was when I was in the depths of my M.E. Being dismissed and misunderstood is a common and overpowering fear for those with M.E. You work hard on such fears, to try to dispel them and then if they become a reality and very openly so, all of that effort and those hopes are dashed. The degree of ignorance and hurt inflicted is immense. The implication is that either those people don't care enough about you full stop, or have not cared enough to take the time to really grasp what your illness is about. Therefore, not only are you spoken to in an extraordinarily dismissive fashion, but people you had hoped may be on your side reveal themselves as being the opposite. Venting their own anger or pain about something and finding you an accessible punchbag, perhaps? That is no justification for inflicting pain on others. It got me to exploring all the things that people do make judgements about and how.

In today's world of course, we have to contend with online prejudice, which can be fierce and cruel. People can so easily express their own distress in the most aggressive forms of attack that they would be far less likely to do in person. Social media has enabled this. I underwent a taster of this type of criticism when I did an interview for *PinkNews*. In talking about my M.E., I uncharacteristically used certain words to explain some of my own experiences of the illness and how at times it had made me feel. It is very common for someone with M.E. to find the extent of your fears so extreme as to verge on paranoia. To believe that threat is not only likely but inevitable. The fight or flight syndrome is heightened hugely. My choice of words was perhaps unfortunate, although I stand by my explanation, and I did apologise for any offence caused. It didn't go down well with many readers who had M.E.. I subsequently learnt from people with personal experience of M.E. who are public figures that they have received death threats. Freedom of speech can be a strange thing.

The song "Don't Judge Me No More" was written from a personal point of view but is hopefully seen as a message on behalf of all people who at times in their lives and for whatever reason have been unfairly judged. It is a plea for people to be less judgmental, more thoughtful and a little more generous towards each other – something we could all do with being.

"In the outward form of sex which the body has assumed, I have remained indifferent, I do not understand the difference between a man and a woman, and believing only in the eternal value of love, I cannot understand these so-called 'normal' people who believe that a man should only love a woman, and woman only love a man.

If this were so, then it disregards completely the spirit, the personality, and the mind, and stresses all the importance of love to the physical body. I believe this is in many cases why the 'normal' people are usually less inspired, seldom artists, and much less sensitive than the 'half-tone' people. They are held down and concerned so much with the physical body that they cannot see beyond the outward form of male and female.

The Greeks understood so well that there is no pure masculine or pure feminine in one person, and in order to bring the body up to the level of the spiritual understanding, they did not hesitate to sculpt on the physical plane the hermaphroditic type in their works of art, and in the poetry of their lives they accepted homo-sexuality and bi-sexuality, whose impulse they regarded as just another stream which flowed toward the same great sea-the eternal source of love."

– Mercedes de Acosta

A Handful of Passions

Shoes

A 6-year-old child sits in front of a villa playing with Sindy and Paul. Creating a make-believe wedding with dolls. The lawn, with its strangely sharp blades of grass, sweeps down to the low wall separating it from the beach. The Spanish sun beams down, caressing everyone in sight. Shorts only for one as young as I. Immersed in my own little world, in the midst of two families going about their holiday business. Inside the house waiting for me are a pair of white leather shoes. Later I will slip into those shoes. Feel the softness of the leather on my bare feet, look down, which being so small isn't far and means that you seem to always be looking up at things and people, and admire their simple beauty and bright whiteness.

Flat leather soles, soft leather uppers. Nothing ostentatious about these shoes. One simple strap, no decorative features. Not shiny white. A sophisticated, cool matt white. And cute. A shoe with a slightly rounded toe that moulded itself to your foot. I don't recall whether I chose them or my mum did, nor how long they survived in such condition and colour. But I adored them. I loved them and still love the memory of them and it was then that I fell in love with shoes. New shoes. Favourite old shoes. Certainly not naff shoes nor ones that don't suit me. Those white shoes suited me.

We were in Marbella. My first foreign holiday. The days before Marbella became the moneyed metropolis that it is now. We had rented the villa where now you will find a gated community. You would need a crane these days to lift you over the gates and into the homes of the celebrated and wealthy. I believe Prince once had a home there. Today, it is a short walk from there to the yachts in the sparkling marina. They are overseen by the Gucci town clock that sits above them and the swathe of designer stores. A far cry from our experience back in 1965. I don't think there were such shops in that exact place then, nor that it would have been where I bought that first most glorious, most treasured and well-remembered pair of shoes.

My next recollection of a pair of shoes that I truly had a passion for, was when I was a little older. My Mother and I, possibly a sibling or two, travelled to Birmingham from our home in Burton upon Trent. We were visiting the department store of the Midlands – Rackhams, and a Ravel shoe shop. I don't recall whether Ravel was a standalone shop or an outlet in the store but it was the Russell & Bromley of its day, or so I understand.

And it was there that I bought the most delicious (this time very shiny) sophisticated and cool, leather soled, flat, black, patent shoes. They went to bed with me that night. Tucked in with me in my lower bunk bed, protecting me from whatever insecurities in my life that now aged 11, I was becoming aware of. Cuddly toys were there too, but these shoes provided all that I needed that night. They made a small child walk tall. They were special and treasured and made me feel both of those things too.

As I have advanced through adulthood, shoes have continued to play an important role in my life. For my self worth, strutting value or simply comfort.

Boots tend to be more my thing now. Chelsea boots. Winkle pickers. Doc Martins. Walking.

I choose carefully. I treat with kindness and respect. I nurture and adore. I've even been known to sing a song about them made famous by Nancy Sinatra – the one with attitude. And the wonderful Paolo Nutini talked about "New Shoes" with some swagger in one of his songs.

New shoes. New boots. Nothing like them. And nothing like them when they're not quite so new but have rather formed themselves around part of your body and in turn have formed part of your personality.

Rolling round full circle, I return to Spain in 2018. And I find some shoes in an obscure shop tucked away in a side street in Granada. Thick rubber soles. Metallic silver lace ups. €9.99 all in. Only one pair there. In my size. They just shouted at me to take them with me. Not a blister to be had, even on the first night wearing them walking down the many cobbled steps from San Antonio Square. Gathering a fan club of desiring people on Facebook. Sitting safely and comfortably on my feet on our return home. Enjoying interest and amusement from fellow passengers going through security and again on the plane. I had much laughter on my 2018 Spanish Odyssey. It was therefore fitting that this continued to the end. And that my shoes got to share in the fun. Oh, what pleasure shoes can bring.

er boots fringe boots jodhpur ankle boots open toe boots drill boots cuban- hee
ots block- heel boots flared-heel boots slim heel boots lace-up boots win
a boots walking boots wellington boots knee high boots steel cap boots
hukka boots riding boots wedge boots suede boots sock boots eng
r ankle boots open toe boots drill boots cuban- **heel boots high-**
heel boots slim heel boots lace-up boots winkle picker boots
ton boots knee high boots steel cap boots hiking boots cow
wedge boots suede boots sock boots engineer boots frin
ots drill boots cuban- **heel boots** high-heel boots block-
ace-up boots winkle picker boots chelsea boots walk
teel cap boots hiking boots cowboy boots chukka
ock boots engineer boots fringe boots jodhpur
ots high-heel boots block- heel boots flared-h
boots chelsea boots walking boots wellingt
cowboy boots chukka boots riding boots
boots jodhpur ankle boots open toe bo
ots flared-heel boots slim heel boot
g boots wellington boots knee high
riding boots wedge boots suede
open toe boots drill boots cuba
slim heel boots lace-up boots
knee high boots steel cap
suede boots sock boots
cuban- heel boots hig
its winkle picker bo
ots hiking boots
engineer boots
eel boots blo
a boots wal
hukka bo
r ankle
heel b
to
N
el boots slin
oots knee hig
edge boots sued
oots drill boots c
oots lace-up boots w
ts steel cap boots hik
ots sock boots engineer
heel boots high-heel boots
picker boots chelsea boots
ts hiking boots cowboy boots
neer boots fringe boots jodhpur
eel boots block- heel boots flared-
chelsea boots walking boots welling
wboy boots chukka boots riding boots
boots jodhpur ankle boots open toe boo
el boots flared-heel boots slim heel boots
ing boots wellington boots knee high boots
oots riding boots wedge boots suede boots soc
kle boots open toe boots drill boots cuban- heel
el boots slim heel boots lace-up boots winkle picker
oots knee high boots steel cap boots hiking boots cov
boots suede boots sock boots engineer boots fringe bo
rill boots cuban- heel boots high-heel boots block- heel b
ace-up boots winkle picker boots chelsea boots walking boo
steel cap boots hiking boots cowboy boots chukka boots ridi
s sock boots engineer boots fringe boots jodhpur ankle boots o
heel boots high-heel boots block- heel boots flared-heel boots slin
picker boots chelsea boots walking boots wellington boots knee hig
king boots cowboy boots chukka boots riding boots wedge boots sue
neer boots fringe boots jodhpur ankle boots open toe boots drill boots
high-heel boots block- heel boots flared-heel boots slim heel boots lace-up
winkle picker boots chelsea boots walking boots wellington boots knee high boots ste
hiking boots cowboy boots chukka boots riding boots wedge boots suede boots sock b
er boots fringe boots jodhpur ankle boots open toe boots drill boots cuban- heel boot

The Avengers

The original Avengers. The cult TV classic. The Emma Peel Years.

> She is the perfect balance of sexiness and sophistication, wit and whimsy. The object of prepubescent lads' desires. Mrs Emma Peel dazzled television screens on both sides of the Atlantic from 1965–1967. Starring Dame Diana Rigg as Peel and Patrick Macnee as John Steed, the Emma Peel era of THE AVENGERS was the high-water mark of the ground-breaking series, with adventures more fantastic than ever.

So, says the blurb on a hard-sought Emma Peel megaset collectors' edition of DVDs. I wasn't aware that there would have been an emphasis on prepubescent lads, or lasses for that matter back in the day, but the rest I would agree with.

I had an absolute fascination with this programme. I still do. It was so far ahead of its time with the storylines, some becoming relevant even only today. The clothes were of their time but sensational. And for me that wit, the humour, nuance and innuendo were out there on their own. Subtle not smutty. Clever. I can watch them over and over again and still be amused, entertained and captivated.

I even wrote a song called "Me and Mrs Peel" and got to sit next to the Dame at a dinner in 2017. On that occasion, I was the one dressed from head to toe in black, almost emulating the look of those 1960s days. For her those times had long gone. But for me and thousands of others, and despite the extraordinary acting she has done since, that role would be the one we will most remember her for.

Writing – *Ikigai*

Ikigai. (生き甲斐,) is a Japanese term for "a reason for being." The word ikigai usually refers to the source of value in one's life or the things that make one's life worthwhile. The word roughly translates to the "thing that you live for" but it also has the nuance of "the reason for which you wake up in the morning" similar to a daily purpose. Each individual's *ikigai* is personal to them and specific to their lives, values and beliefs. It reflects the inner self of an individual and expresses that faithfully, while simultaneously creating a mental state in which the individual feels at ease. Activities that allow one to feel *ikigai* are never forced on an individual; they are often spontaneous, and always undertaken willingly, giving the individual satisfaction and a sense of meaning to life. – Wikipedia.

Writing is my *ikigai.*

Health

"You can't see everything going on in a body or a mind."

Below is a summary of all the illnesses and conditions I have had in my life that I can remember or know of. Dates in most cases are accurate, in some approximate. I have always had a natural interest in health, perhaps because I come from a medical family, perhaps because I chose a career in preventative health when I was a young woman. Over the last 8 years, I started to become interested in how those things could be linked. In the last couple of years, as my health has improved and I have perhaps become more self-aware and less self-critical, I have been able to be more objective. I consulted two health practitioners to seek out their professional opinions. Sections from the transcripts of those conversations follow.

1. Childhood. German measles twice. A bad dose of chicken pox, which a GP likened to smallpox.

2. Age 18/19. Anorexia/exercise bulimia. Initially I used laxatives but then became obsessive about exercise. I was playing county hockey, was school games captain, working out in a gym, walking everywhere and eating healthily but as things escalated, I stopped eating in the evening. The cause is unknown. I can't recall what I was thinking or trying to achieve. I don't remember my body image being one I didn't like. My weight went down to 7 stone from 10 1/2. This happened during a year when I was retaking an A level. I had been rejected by a woman who I had fallen in love with. Being unsure of my sexuality, I didn't feel able to share this with anyone. It resulted in not getting the A level results needed to get into my college of choice and I had to stay at school for an extra year to achieve that. Having clashed with my dad, who I had been living with for several years following the family break up when I was 13, I was back living in our old family home with my mum who was going through a very difficult time.

3. Aged 22. Glandular fever. Bed bound for 5 weeks at my mum and stepfather's home. Throat likened to diphtheria. Couldn't swallow. Fed through straw. Lost over 1 stone in weight. I was depressed to the point where I told Mum I wanted out. My body ached constantly. My spleen was affected and I wasn't allowed to drink alcohol for 6 months once I was up and about again. This illness developed in the run up to my finals. My personal life was in disarray due to my closeted sexuality. I remained at college for an extra year to gain my degree.

4. Age 26. Tonsillectomy.

5. Age 32. Lumpectomy. Fibroadenoma. A stubborn lump in a series of cysts. One aspiration didn't clear. One I ignored. But one that my parents, once I informed them insisted and made arrangements to get sorted out. A scary and tense two weeks. Trips up to my hometown to see the consultant, to have the operation, to get the results. And relief. The thought of the thing that it wasn't a thing that gives me the terrors.

6. Age 28+. Insomnia. Became very acute in my 40s. I juggled this alongside some demanding jobs – chiefly waking up around 3am having slept from 11-12 pm and then staying awake until 5 or 6am. Alarm would go off at 6.30am. In the early days, I would read during those waking hours. Listen to music. Work. Curiously, those times can be very creative. Some of my best ideas were developed during wakeful night-time hours in my employed years, initially for planning and developing, later for writing creatively. At times, I would get very distressed when not going back to sleep. I have used most herbal pills and teas, meditations, reading, listening to music, getting up and walking around, or sitting and reflecting. I have tried acupuncture and yoga. I have employed most sleep hygiene factors. In 2009, I started using sleeping pills, which I use in moderation to this day along with adjusting my lifestyle, in some ways out of necessity. When I went to see an endocrinologist in 2010, before M.E. was diagnosed a year later, his conclusion was that my sleeping issues were at the root of my health issues.

7. Early 40s. I recognised that I possibly had low blood sugar issues. Although never officially diagnosed, this was considered highly likely by a renowned and highly regarded homeopath who I went to see because of continuous health issues that couldn't be explained by visits to my GP. I adjusted my dietary habits to try and manage this more effectively.

8. Age 42. Perimenopause. 10 years earlier than average.

9. Age 44. Toxoplasmosis diagnosed. When seeking help for my perimenopausal challenges, I underwent tests at King's College Hospital, London, and this was unexpectedly discovered. The symptoms are not dissimilar to glandular fever and M.E.

10. Age 44. Broke my ankle. I was on crutches for 6 weeks non-weight bearing.

11. Age 47. Menopausal issues reached a peak. Flushes were extreme and emotions high. I experienced severe anxiety, especially in the morning. I would wake up curled up in a ball. I had chronic and acute digestive problems. I was reluctant to go on Hormone Replacement Therapy (HRT). I was given Diazepam to combat the anxiety. I went to a women's clinic who suggested that low blood sugar was the main cause of the anxiety and that I probably had Candidiasis and parasites. All were proved correct through tests. I started using natural supplements and tinctures and adjusted my diet. The transformation was marked.

12. Age 51. December 2010, I had a nasty flu-like virus that I couldn't shake off. I had damaged the same ankle that I had broken a few years earlier and was again on crutches for 6 weeks. I was putting myself under a lot of pressure.

13. Age 52. November 2011, M.E. was diagnosed. A mild diagnosis, not moderate or severe. M.E. is known as an invisible illness. Other people can't see it. It isn't obvious like a broken arm or perhaps a heavy cold. And when someone with M.E. is very poorly they won't be out in public or choose to be in company anyway. Throughout 2011, my health issues had escalated: persistent, overwhelming and unexplained periods of severe fatigue. Flu-like symptoms. Aching/squirmy muscles. Occasional electric headaches. Digestive issues. Very poor sleep. Irritable skin. Palpitations. Fuzzy head. Vertigo. Big emotional issues with a very heightened stress response. Poor concentration. Short term memory problems. Light/noise intolerance.

My experience of M.E. is as follows. Trivial tasks such as writing an email or making a bed would be mentally and physically exhausting. I heard someone say that she balled her eyes out when she couldn't fit a fork in the dishwasher. That's the sort of level of stress response you can get with M.E.. Stress of any form would then trigger physical symptoms such as digestive pain and discomfort, aching muscles, irritable skin, headaches, and ultimately result in fatigue that compares to no other form. Your battery is empty and you have nothing on standby. The default of your thought patterns is likely to be negative a lot of the time. Fears feature heavily. It is as likely that physical symptoms start without a stress trigger and for no apparent reason.

Undertaking tasks on a day when you feel well and find those hard to resist, would mean being exhausted the day afterwards. I have taken many risks knowing this but finding the temptation too great. In the first 2 to 3 years of my illness when it was at its worst, I still had a good degree of fitness. I even remember swimming 24 lengths once, resulting in being in bed for the next 2 days. Now I only manage 12 although I'm building on that. Whilst my health has improved, my fitness has regressed.

I would wear dark glasses a lot of the time, not to be cool but to minimise the effects of bright lights or the overwhelming sensory overload caused by sound, light, and groups or crowds of people. If you have a fuzzy, vertiginous head, driving 2 miles down the road is likely to be as exhausting and as great an impossibility as driving from Land's End to John O'Groats. And is likely to be highly unsafe not only for you, but for other road users.

On bad days, moving further than the bedroom to the lounge was not possible physically. It would also have been a painfully daunting and overwhelming experience, especially if it involved interaction with people. Social interaction was exhausting, with many hours being spent taking myself away to a quiet room, or even to bed to be alone when other people are in our house or when we were visiting the homes of others. In the early days, this was enormously upsetting.

I continue to have to make many choices about what I can do or take on even just on a daily basis. I have to be more considered than most healthy people of my age. I have made many mistakes where these decisions are concerned and there have been many repercussions. There still are but as long as I can try and factor those things in, the disappointment is lessened, and I now have a very good quality of life.

M.E. has severely limited my capacity to do many things. But it has also changed and shaped my life, sometimes in very positive ways. I had to stop doing many things like earning a living because I couldn't sustain employment. I had to stop performing, having only just started. But because of it I started writing a journal. Not a diary of events, but a record of my thoughts and feelings. This in turn led to me writing poems, which in many cases became song lyrics. It gave me permission to know that I didn't have to always be doing something. This gave me time and space and a head clear enough to reflect and be more measured and creative. I also recognise that I have been fortunate in being able to afford to seek help when there has been no NHS support on offer.

I do not undermine the enormous struggles M.E. has brought me. I am also keen not to undermine those who have suffered more with this illness and have illnesses that may be deemed more serious.

14. Age 55. Very high cholesterol detected. When blood tests were done initially for cholesterol we also tested for the Epstein–Barr virus. Apparently, there had been a recent flare up. This could have been the virus that had triggered M.E. in December of 2010. Had I known, would I have lived my life differently? Would M.E. have developed? My cholesterol has now returned to normal.

15. Age 58. In February 2017, Seasonal Affective Disorder (SAD) was diagnosed after two especially difficult winters. This was over a period of time when some family matters had become very damaging. It is thought now that I have a tendency to get reactive depression, meaning that when I am facing prolonged and very difficult situations, I can get depressed. I think I have always had a leaning towards this. To combat these things, I use a low dose selective serotonin reuptake inhibitor anti-depressant (SSRI). I did use a light box and spent a long period in early 2018 in a brighter country. I have used counselling for M.E. for many years and continue to dip into techniques taken from cognitive behavioural therapy, mindfulness and other recognised therapies. Last year I also decided that I had to distance myself from the things and people that had been having a negative impact upon my mental health.

16. Age 59. Right cataract operated on. I went on statins. Leaking cholesterol in my left eye having been spotted. Taking statins was delayed because it was considered that they may impact negatively on my already challenged immune system.

Conversation between Jude and Lisa Smith, Nutritionist. Lisa has worked with me since 2012.

L: My theory is that when you're looking at anorexia and M.E. and you take the character traits of those people, they are very similar. My theory is: what goes first? The mind or the body? When you're younger, the mind gives first and that's the eating disorder. When you're older and a little bit more experienced and you can be more rational, it's the body that gives. Those traits are: perfectionist, high achiever.

J: Being determined to the point of being stubborn!

L: A lot of my experience of anorexia is very black and white. For whatever the reason the anorexia is there, it isn't necessarily the food or a need to be thin and society and pressure, that isn't it at all. This raises the question of whether these traits are nature or nurture, which is a matter that a psychologist can throw light on. I think both anorexia and any chronic fatigue (M.E.) are both people's heightened sensitivities to life. So your hormones and neurotransmitters all fluctuate and it's not necessarily that these people have bigger fluctuations, it's that their bodies don't deal with the fluctuations they do have. The body and mind then don't deal with extremes.

J: I've always maintained that I had a virus, which was one of the physical triggers for M.E.. I also very definitely say that M.E. is a mind and body meltdown really. There might be numerous triggers that set it off because it's like an explosion. I was putting myself under a lot of pressure with a number of different things, so my mind and my body got to a point where it couldn't keep taking that bombardment.

L: There comes a point where your self-preservation is just in shut-down.

J: I suppose going back to the anorexia/bulimia, that was because I was very, very hurt. I'd come through some very difficult years with my parents splitting up and not getting on with my dad, so it was quite a lot of disruption really. And then there was all the sexuality stuff, which I was having to keep suppressed. When you do that to your body physically - and I've only got life experience to go on - you're abusing your body by starving it or whatever. That can't really set you up very well for making you robust.

L: I always think when I'm doing a talk to people training to be anorexia therapists: all those years of calorie restriction, there's a deficit being made. All the things that would've been going on, on an ongoing basis.

J: Mine was quite short-lived compared to lots of people.

L: It was still during the time when you were developing and growing. Even if it was for 6 months, those 6 months without sufficient nutrients to repair and heal - and at a time when you're excessively exercising? You're damaging yourself.

J: I was. I would say - again, with the knowledge I have - it started out as anorexia but very quickly became exercise bulimia because I became obsessive about exercise. So, I was absolutely punishing my body with what I was putting it through, without having the fuel going in.

L: That's it; you then acquire this deficit. Just eating normally again isn't necessarily going to correct this deficit. In order for the body to cope, it changes into third gear. However, what happens then, if you try driving in third gear, you'll know that you're revving a lot, you're not going fast but you're wearing out the car. So unless the body is looked after sufficiently, you won't get back. Then glandular fever- as soon as you see M.E., you ask, "Have you had glandular fever?" The glandular fever would have kept you in third gear. This is the thing - that you don't deal well with extremes because the body can't.

J: And yet my mind would be in first gear, overdrive. Because of the personality traits you mention, that would be going hell for leather relatively speaking, compared to what my body could cope with.

L: I've probably said to you that if I had to describe chronic fatigue (M.E.) in a sentence, it's taking twice as long to make half the energy. You may be able to do the exercise - chronic fatigue can do the exercise - but has a very slow recovery. Being in third gear, taking twice as long to make half the energy means that the repair doesn't happen. Say you do try and do something and use your muscles, they don't get repaired efficiently, lactic acid builds up, that adds to the aches and the pains. Every time you do something, it's one step forward, two steps back. That's where you have this period when people are wiped out and bedridden because at least they're not exerting themselves then and can give the body a little bit of a catch-up. Having said that, the backlog and deficits makes it very hard for the body to catch up fully. These aren't the sort of things you can test for. It's not, "You're a bit low in zinc and magnesium." You might be on a day-to-day basis but it's the body's reserves that are depleted.

J: Looking at this from a very objective point of view, which I can do now, I just find it fascinating. I can see how all these things have had a knock-on effect, right from that nineteen-year-old who was punishing herself in that way to when we were living in London and toxoplasmosis was diagnosed. I was packed off to all sorts of places and specialists because I was clearly having quite a lot of challenges with energy. Marg and I were very convinced that I had blood sugar issues. I went to see a specialist who said, "I'm absolutely certain you have low blood sugar." There was lots of evidence that pointed to that with my behaviour or my coping mechanisms throughout my 40s and earlier. I absolutely see how they would be completely interlinked.

L: If I had one word for a common thing throughout everything written here, it's stress but let's redefine that, not as worry. Stress is anything that puts a demand on the body and that means the body has to make an adjustment to stay in balance. If you look at all of those things you've been through, and had wrong with you, they've been putting a demand on your body. That's where the issue is because the reserves weren't there to allow you to cope. Your body's physical adaptation had been reduced

J: I like going and staying in huts and things. Maybe I'm not cut out by nature for the 21st century!

L: Exactly. You get away from the toxins, the noise, all of those things, the constant TV and phones; there's no switch off. You don't necessarily have, at a physical level, the adaptive qualities to cope with that without getting a symptom. Symptoms are because we have too little or too much of something in the body. It doesn't take a big imbalance for you to have a symptom. But that makes the problem harder to find because it isn't a red flag showing you have too much or too little of something, it's more subtle than that. That's why things like dental work and anaesthetics for example, make you really wired and jittery, because it's another demand and pressure. Again, the body is struggling to maintain balance because it's never really managed to from the start. Then you would've had puberty to deal with so you're still stabilising from that. When I'm talking to people who have had eating disorders there's a sensitivity coupled with an ability to take things on. But you also need a lot of stimulation. You're just the way you are but your body is going,

---

"Dear God, Jude!"

J: It's quite interesting. When I set my cap at this current album and book project and was discussing things to be done with Marg she said, "You could just put your feet up and enjoy life!"

L: There are lots of people who would just think, "I can't be bothered. It's too much hassle."

J: Marg was very adamant that I enjoy this process and ensure it doesn't become, "I've said I'm going to do that and I'm going to deliver that there, so therefore I'm going to make it happen." It needs to be a pleasurable experience and not just seeking to achieve something. With my first album I put myself under enormous pressure.

L: There comes a point when even good pressure or stress is stress. All the things written here in some way or another are putting a demand on your body. My thing is that you never had those back-up of reserves; from your anorexia/bulimic stage, you almost went straight into glandular fever. Do you ever recover from GF if it's severe? I don't know. As soon as you get under stress and your immune gets stressed, it's allowed to come out and play; that's why it follows periods of stress because the energy dips. Going back to you saying that your anorexia was mild, it wasn't if you consider what your coping mechanisms are, remember? It might on paper look mild, but to a body suffering it, it isn't.

> "Your 59-year-old self needs to listen to the advice in this conversation and take heed too." Marg Mayne

Marg has encouraged me in my projects, but has been a reassuring presence and voice at all times when my health has struggled. Helping me to tune in to myself, heeding the signs when I don't. At times during the height of my M.E., it was very hard for both of us. We worry understandably about the health and happiness of those closest to us. At that time, a very demanding job kept Marg in London during the week, meaning that she wasn't at hand when she felt I needed her to be and likewise I wasn't able to support her as much as I would have liked. It is important to do what we can for each other and to look after ourselves to give ourselves the best shot at that.

Conversation between Jude and Ashok Gupta, Clinic Director, the Gupta Programme. I used this M.E. recovery programme from 2012 to assist with management of my M.E.

A: The way we're living now is very different to the way we have over millennia. Combined with that, we are experiencing different types of stress. The first time a child is exposed to stress is actually in the womb. The levels of stress that a mother has impacts on the levels of stress that a child has.

Essentially, stress is a protective mechanism. So, stress, fear, anxiety – these are defence mechanisms. We see them as emotions, like stress or fear being an emotion, but actually it's a defence mechanism from the system. When the system is exposed to environments it's not used to in the modern world, that defence mechanism goes into overdrive. Then that defence mechanism if it's not delicately balanced, can cause more problems than the things it's trying to defend the body from.

Our factory setting, defence mechanism or how defensive we are towards the environment, is first of all determined by our parents' levels of anxiety, especially our mother's levels in the womb. If the birth experience is very traumatic or long then that can also impact on the defensive nature of the brain, especially the brain structure called the amygdala, which is our defensive mechanism. Finally, our upbringing, so the first 10-15 years of our lives can impact heavily on the factory setting of our amygdala, and not just our amygdala but our immune responses.

The modern-day world medicine treats it as either a defensive mechanism or an emotional defence mechanism. But actually, they are completely one and the same because the brain isn't differentiating between one being an emotional condition and one being a physical condition. And so, then what happens is what we call a sensitive personality type, but we don't mean sensitive purely from an emotional perspective but from the whole person – mentally, physically, emotionally and spiritually. People who have this sensitivity are often very connected to the arts because they have that sensitivity to life, to the arts, to poetry, to music. So, it's interesting that you're a songwriter. They can be sensitive to people around them. It's not saying a sensitive personality trait is anything wrong or bad – it has its upsides and downsides.

You mentioned your background anorexia. We know that this is a fear-based response in the brain to what it sees as danger. That danger might be the way you are perceived; body dysmorphia comes from that, the dangers of putting on weight in any shape or form. That is very much connected to, once again, a defence mechanism in the brain which might explain some of that tendency.

Then you've mentioned glandular fever. Now we know that our defence mechanisms are finely tuned to protect us against disease - viruses and bacteria. If we are too stressed and we've got that predisposition and then we're going through university, which is the first time when we're on our own and we don't have our parents to look after us. It is also the first time we are exposing ourselves and our personality to the people around us, and that can mean that our finely tuned immune system can't defend effectively against pretty aggressive glandular fever, which is why a lot of people at university get this illness. It can affect them quite severely, because our system with all the stress, the bad eating, the late nights, the partying -these all affect our immune system and the ability to fight off infection and means we can have a more severe reaction to things like glandular fever.

Then, combined with that, is insomnia. A sensitive personality trait will find it harder to have deeper sleep, good quality of sleep. It's because when the brain is in a heightened state of continual alert, why would it want you to sleep? It would want you to deal with potential dangers. Once again, it's a predisposition genetically combined with a predisposition based on nature and nurture. So all of the things that affect our lifestyle can impact on our ability to handle our environments. Insomnia to me, is the brain's natural reaction to an environment which is mentally, emotionally or physically stressful and it's obviously more associated with stress.

Then you've mentioned low blood sugar levels, or hypoglycaemia, which can also be as a result of a system which isn't operating correctly and can have lots of ups and downs. Low and high blood sugar levels can operate with highs and lows of the emotional type as well. I'd love to hear your view on the emotional type and emotional experiences you had while you were having low blood sugar issues. The other things could be incidental. You've also mentioned setting up a business, a new career in interior design and singing.

J: There was so much going on at that time. It was crazy really, when I look back. Any one of those things would've been a huge undertaking in terms of what you're referring to and my levels of sensitivity. I think we can go back to the nature/nurture thing because you've mentioned that and it was certainly something that Lisa really tapped into big time. I grew up feeling that I was expected to take it all on. My Dad used to call me The Mighty Jude and that kind of sums it up. I wish I'd said now, "I'm not so mighty, actually!" But then you live up to that and so you just think, "Bring it all on. I can deal with this and that," and you just go into overload.

A: It's really interesting that you mention that because certainly when we're treating M.E., chronic fatigue syndrome and fibromyalgia there seem to be certain personality traits that spring up. If you have a sensitive personality trait, combined with one of these other personality traits, such as the achiever, the helper and the approval seeker, then that magnifies everything.

This is already somebody who finds dealing with a challenging environment more tricky, and needs to take care of their health more than before. But actually, they're less likely to take care of their health because of the expectations they place on themselves, based on a ghost voice of the parent. The Mighty Jude may well be an achiever trait, which means, "Yes, I'm going to do interior design, run a boutique B&B, start singing." It's taking on so much because there's an element of mainly needing to justify my existence to myself but more to the world around me through achieving, proving myself, getting people's admiration. There's nothing wrong with that but the issue is does it make us unconsciously ignore our health?

Sensitive personality trait people need even more self-care than the average person in the street. Maybe they don't really look after themselves, which then triggers a condition. So, you then get a virus or bacteria and the body thinks, "Okay, I can handle this virus even though I'm exhausted. I'll fight it off." But if the brain thinks that it's only just managing to fight this off, then it will go into overdrive mode and any small symptoms that mimic the presence of the virus, will overstimulate the immune system and the nervous system. It's an overprotective response, which is a perfectly normal and natural thing to do from an evolutionary perspective. But from a health perspective it keeps you in a permanent state of overstimulation.

So, it's essentially a protective system which is overprotecting to ensure survival. M.E. doesn't feel good but as far as the brain is concerned, it is erring on the side of caution. Then you get opportunistic viruses and infections – you mentioned Epstein Barr. It sounds counterintuitive, but the brain is just doing the best it can. I think that, combined with this as I said, what makes it worse is the achiever, helper and approval seeker. There's nothing wrong with that or something that we regret but it then means that that self-care, which is so important with these conditions, is often put to the back burner as we focus on gaining whatever we feel is necessary.

J: I think I'm all three of those things. I think for me the anorexia really kicked things off. Within 3 years I had glandular fever. One of the many things I did to help with my M.E. was to start journaling and then it turned into poetry and I thought there were possibly some song lyrics in there. I've never played an instrument or anything but I was coming up with tunes and so they evolved. Then what do I have to do? I have to turn it into an album. I can't be satisfied with just writing some nice songs for myself! It turned into this huge project.

Now I'm undertaking another big project in a much more measured way, admittedly, and I have the benefit of experience of having made one album. There were some hugely challenging times in making that album when I really wasn't well. It's just like, "What the hell have I taken on?" But the achiever just had to do it and see it through. Even the launch was a multimedia extravaganza. I'm very confident that I'm approaching this current project in a different way. The process is going to be very enjoyable with less of a focus on the sort of product at the end. Although, of course, I want the product at the end to be very special.

Also, when you said something about the nature/nurture thing earlier on? Fundamentally I like simple things in life but with society and my upbringing, the achiever and some of these other things, I've put myself in situations that probably aren't natural to me. So. I love taking myself off. There's nothing I love more - to camp or to stay in a very basic shepherd's hut on my own. Solitude, no electricity or running water, taking it right back to what you were saying about the hunter/ gatherer environment. But the reality of life isn't like that and we try to build more around us and take on more activities and responsibilities and commitments and so forth. Really, I should be living in a hut, shouldn't I? Then I probably would never have had any of these issues but that's never going to happen.

A: I remember there was a client of mine who picked up a book on M.E. and the very first line of the book was, "M.E. is about understanding the root cause of your condition and not loving yourself enough." She got so freaked out by this sentence that she closed the book and threw it away and didn't go back to it. If we look at songs that are written, songs that have depth, ultimately everything is about love.

The core theme of any narrative, whether it be poetry or music or prose, for me it's about discovering and understanding that we are already loved or loveable or it's a narrative about expressing that love to others. Self-love, self-acceptance, a self-appreciation. When people feel more of that, they naturally have better health and are naturally better at handling the environment because it's coming from a genuine place of self-love and not just a surface level of self-love. Once we truly get to that stage of deep self-acceptance, we can say to ourselves, "There's nothing I have to do or prove. I am complete in this moment right now." That's when the nervous system will breathe a deep sigh of relief and come down a few notches. Our system will then maintain more of a balance. That then expresses itself in the arts, so we have a lot of people who are recovering from the condition and they spontaneously feel they want to write poetry or a song because it's the transformation from a caterpillar into a butterfly.

J: It's a freedom. It's a freedom because you have given yourself permission. It's a freedom because you're not under that pressure and bombarding yourself with all of those things. It's also then a release for all of the deep-seated feelings that then manifest themselves in lots of different ways.

A: One word you gave is absolutely key: "permission" to be me. "I give myself permission to be me and just be. Anything else is a bonus". This idea of, "I've got all the love inside of me. Anything else is a bonus. Anything else is nice to have." If we can get to that place, then everything becomes a lot easier and our nervous system and immune system come back to their natural selves and natural setting. That's also combined with silence; when we feel that sense of self-love, we can crave silence and stillness in nature and getting away from it all because the modern, city environment encourages and feeds the ego self or the sense of, "I need to prove myself in some way or my self-image," whereas living in a hut in the middle of nowhere gives us permission to just be with nature and commune with nature, be more natural and be in the stillness and silence, which is why the key to this, for me, is regular meditation. When our clients regularly meditate, it gradually soothes the sense of trying to use the world to justify what our existence is; it soothes it down and they get a sense of being and how lovely that feels, that permission.

J: I did have a lot of headspace and that sense of freedom and peace, which is probably why I was writing quite a lot. Out of that, I sort of extracted the songs that went on the album. Because that was quite a while ago, in many ways things have evolved and my health has improved. I've still got a little way to go. I do have to tune into myself and pull myself up sometimes to feel that sense of freedom and peace again to allow myself to write freely and creatively and especially because I'm partly spending time writing a memoir, which is about memory; it's not strictly speaking about creating things out of nowhere, though I do want to write and create the book as creatively as possible.

So it's quite interesting because I need to be careful not to slip back into old habits where I'm not giving myself the time, the freedom, the

———————

space, the peace, if you like, to let all that stuff flow out. Over the next few months, especially, that's going to be very important because that's when I need to be really focused on writing and not worrying about scheduling social media stuff. I have a lot of the project planned and already organised because that's very necessary and all these applications for funding and all that. I need to get out of that side of my brain and just free things up a little bit. That's going to be very, very important. It'll go full circle because it'll be very important for my creativity but that will be good for my health, which will in turn help the whole process.

A: I agree with that. I think the creative process itself is hindered when we are attached to a particular result or outcome. Most of the way we bring up children is actually about the joys and the outcome. The joy comes before the outcome. It's about loving what you do rather than getting a particular outcome. In the same way the actual joy of writing/ singing creatively is itself the pleasure and anything else that comes out of it in terms of recognition or other people loving what you're doing, once again, if seen as a bonus rather than the core of it then that fills the creative need.

"Moderation is not my middle name. The M just stands for Mary."
Jude Adams

Night Thinker

My body's excited
Legs squirmy, twitchy, aches.
My head's wide awake
Despite pills, radio, I meditate.

My love sleeps beside me
Soft breaths in and out.
Oblivious to my waking
To my heart rate as it pounds.

How long will I lie here working hard for slumber.
What hour will it be until it casts aside it's fears
Gives in to the rhythms of the night
Until in the morning things become clear.

Melancholic
Why don't you go home now
I'm feeling alone now
Having you here.
Melancholic
Why don't you go home now
I'm feeling so low now
Having you near.

Travel

Ben and Jerry

A return to a Greek island, Spetses, was very welcome in 1997. Marg started to write a novelette about the other Brits we met. One couple, for some unknown reason that we nicknamed Ben and Jerry, seemed to pop up wherever we went. They were staying in the same quite intimate apartment complex to which they returned every year. It transpired quite early in our stay that they came from Swadlincote, just outside my hometown. Despite this, we didn't encourage much conversation, but as we sat minding our own business one day, reading and taking in the sun, their curiosity got the better of them. "How's the novel coming along Marg? Are you writing about us?!" Their enquiry was jovial. Little did they know. Despite our employing a number of avoidance techniques, Ben and Jerry were a constant. One day we cycled miles to a secluded beach only to see their heads bobbing in the water as we came over the brow of a hill. "This cannot be flipping possible," I said as Marg shrieked, "Bloody hell. Maybe they're stalking us!" We scarpered. A perfectly delightful couple but escape was necessary. Marg never did finish her novelette but they did make it into a book.

Relationships

I woke one night at 3.30am. Not an uncommon occurrence. I had been having a vivid and curious dream. Aren't they always. It was initially a happy dream, but it quickly turned quite sour and I think, stirred in me some dark, brooding reminder of the sadness and surprise there can be in relationships. The realisation that dawns that you have been duped, that laughter has been cut short, the smile taken from your eyes.

The worst type of relationships are those where you feel like you've been dropped into a deep sack around the neck of which, the tie has been tightened. You are squirming around, pushing against the sides, prodding, poking, kicking, flailing but you are helpless to find a way out. It has you trapped like Houdini's worst nightmare. And you feel the deceit. The provider of your freedom, the giver of life and your happiness, circling outside with such simple power at their fingertips. But no desire to share it.

Such relationships can be manifested in different circumstances. Lover. Spouse. Parent. Child. Sibling. Friend. Work.

The best relationships are the ones that are unconditional or as good as. "Like a lover who cares", they should set you free, relinquishing selfish needs and wants to ensure happiness for the other person. Made up of respect, generosity of spirit, and of tolerance. Making you feel you can fly, flourish, be strong, safe, satisfied, empowered, remarkable.

Girls and boys come out to play

I had my first boyfriend when I was about 10. His family and mine were staying at the Tenby House Hotel in Pembrokeshire where my staple diet was consommé and steak and chips. He wore a white skinny rib polo neck as did I. And he took me to the zoo and bought me chocolate buttons.

Amongst a series of boyfriends during my youth, from borstal boy skinheads and muscle-bound rugby players to public schoolboys and many other crushes and snatched fumbles, there was another boyfriend with the same name as the one who had taken me to the zoo. We dated for a good 18 months when I was a mere 15. He was adorable. Charming, clever, sensitive and mature beyond his years. His father and stepmother were friends of my parents. I think I broke his heart. I didn't mean to, but I think I did.

Over the ensuing years I know that I hurt other partners and was hurt in return by some. For my part in any of those things I am truly sorry. Sometimes I and they have apologised, other times not.

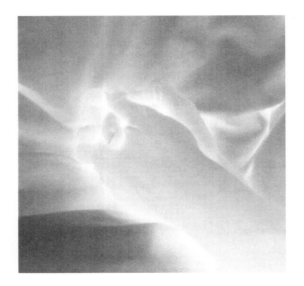

My Wife

THERE IS NO POEM,

THERE ARE NO WORDS,

SHE IS MY LIFE,

'TIS ALL.

Into the deep

The First Cut

I fell deeply in love for the first time when I was 18. I was in a steady relationship with another wonderful boy who seemingly had all the qualities a nice middle-class girl like me could wish for and need. Good looks, a good brain, sporty, sensitive, good prospects, a motorbike! And a hopeless devotion to me. But I had thoughts and feelings about other things at that time. I had met someone who name dropped about famous people, whose accent held no hints of Staffordshire and who had, to me, a deeply attractive, rebellious streak. This rebellious streak didn't appeal to many but amused me greatly. I befriended this "blow in" from the snooty South who appeared to have experiences of a world beyond our own. Experiences that I was hungry for.

And this person was a woman. A potentially dangerous liaison indeed.

Having long recognised that I was pulled physically and emotionally towards both sexes, I did believe that any attraction I had for women was likely to be a phase. Wasn't that always the case when you were a teenager? Surely only PE teachers and women who wore terribly sensible shoes were the only women who were really allowed to be lesbians? Lipstick lesbians hadn't been invented in 1977, as far as I know or knew of, in my somewhat closeted hometown. As a footnote, I may add that I still feel uncomfortable using that word, which I rarely do because of the stigma and association often attached to it.

Until this time, I had enjoyed the attentions, affections, company and pleasures of teenage lust and love with the opposite sex. The difference with the feelings I was developing now, was that this wasn't Virginia Wade or Dusty Springfield – immensely talented women suspected of being of another persuasion. Women to be admired and fantasised about from pictures in a magazine, on TV or out of the speakers of my record player. This was a real life, walking, talking woman who I was forming a very close friendship with and feelings for.

To explain why we are attracted to certain people is almost an impossibility and only something we can speculate about. Beauty is in the eye of the beholder but even if something is not to your personal taste, you may still acknowledge it. Fascination with someone's personality can be understandable to many but may manifest itself in stronger emotions amongst a few. Connecting with someone is a comfortable, enticing, sometimes exciting feeling. Whether you have the ability to chat easily with someone, make each other laugh without hesitation, have similar interests or perhaps even similar social backgrounds that draw you together. Or a collection of things. Or quite simply chemistry.

I really hadn't reckoned with what lay ahead. Perhaps I felt safe in the knowledge that this sort of thing couldn't possibly happen to me. Any feelings I had ever had for someone of my own sex were regarded by myself as a distant fantasy, as something totally out of bounds, off limits and out of the question. Just not something that I perceived was or could be a reality. And did I even know for sure that it was something that I wanted anyway? Wasn't it something to be got over, that would blow away in time?

Whatever the reason and there are always likely to be many, it is safe to say that I was smitten. The feelings I had for this person were ones that I naively believed were being kept to myself and allowed to flow. However, these feelings brought me up abruptly several months into our friendship when, with a significant amount of Dutch courage, I chose unwisely (as it turned out) to reveal them to her.

Having already become friends, we were limited in how much time we spent together. We both had boyfriends and other commitments. The romantic feelings evolved in a very short space of time. Then one evening at her house, we were lounging around in her sitting room chatting, listening to music, no-one else home. I don't recall if it was a weekend, or whether we had been out, nor whether it was early or late. I have a recollection that she was sober. I wasn't. Whether as a deliberate act or because I had set my mind at what I had to say or do, I can't say. And then I took leave of my senses and shared my feelings. It was all over very quickly. Whatever it was I said came as a jolt to me as much as I imagine it did to her, and her response was calm but clear. "I think you've had quite a lot to drink, Jude. Perhaps you should go home now." A kind rebuff but given the depth of feelings I had, the courage it had taken me to open myself up, and the enormity of what was to follow, to me it felt very unkind. I felt a complete fool. I maintain to this day that she was not at fault because I don't think she had any real knowledge or understanding of my feelings, my bravery and what the fallout might be. I didn't know myself.

If someone has no understanding of your feelings, then they could be said to be free from any responsibility regarding any outcomes and that you are alone in managing those feelings for yourself. If the other person has some level of knowledge or understanding of feelings you have towards them, or suspects you have, then if they are a responsible, respectful, caring person they would surely act in a way to negate any harm. But that is a very idealistic way to look at the world and not in reality what happens. People can hurt each other in so many ways, directly or indirectly by words and deeds, sometimes unwittingly and, in more unpleasant circumstances, knowingly. I know there is at least one person (almost the only person who recognised what was happening to me at this time) who might argue that the woman I had fallen for knew full well what was happening. That I was falling in love with her or at the least had a very serious crush on her and that she had led me on. I don't know. I would like to disagree, but I am conscious that I tend to look upon people kindly even when they may be hurting me. Is this arrogance that you believe someone wouldn't hurt you intentionally or just a belief in the greater good of humanity? I hope the latter. She may have flirted and perhaps had an inkling, but to her that was her nature. It was part of her make up. Something she perhaps knew I enjoyed because it was part of our friendship; living a little dangerously. Teasing. Having a laugh. Not something she had the vaguest idea about in terms of what it could really mean.

We were young but that is not to take any of this lightly. Feelings can be very deep and very real even at that tender age and relationships and their intensity need to be taken seriously. I was also more vulnerable than I have often given myself credit for and that wasn't on view to the outside world. A strong willed, determined, fun loving, slightly difficult teenager to many. And whilst I was that person, I was also sensitive to, and troubled by, years of family turmoil. In addition, there were the confused emotions regarding my possible sexuality. I was muddling through in a family and society where sharing your problems on any level was not encouraged nor indulged. Let us also not forget that these early experiences can determine your later behaviours and form a mind map for your future health and happiness.

A levels came and went.

My deep hurt and humiliation were suppressed and damaging. We were adult enough to maintain a good show of friendship, this incident never ever being mentioned or alluded to, as though it had never happened. Studying for my imminent exams was a struggle. Not a natural academic, I was distracted and tended to ruminate for hours on end. I continued for a short while in the relationship with my boyfriend until I had to bring that to a close. In his distress, he proclaimed that he thought I'd rather spend time with "her". Naturally, I denied it but of course knew it to be the truth. If I couldn't have a romantic relationship with this woman then I certainly still preferred to spend time with her more than almost anyone else. Very grown up but also a choice that was not going to give my wounds a chance to heal.

I was by now drinking quite a lot of red wine and smoking heavy duty French cigarettes, unable to explain why to my mother and one of my sisters on the one occasion that they tried to engage with me about it. Cocooned with my pain and confusion, more often than not in a locked bedroom listening to music. Biding my time until I could escape to London to the prestigious West London Institute of Education (Borough Sports College) and a new life and shake off these feelings and this situation.

Then the A level results came. Not to make light of it, which often I do, that moment happened to coincide with hearing that one of my idols, Elvis Presley, had died. Apart from the Osmonds and all the usual pop icons of the time, I was a huge fan of the more mature Beatles, Dusty, and the King. Having received that news through my transistor radio and realising what day it was, I pottered slightly apprehensively downstairs to pick up the post. And opened the letter. I got a D in Religious Studies. And either failed or got a totally unexpected and unsatisfactory grade in Art, and English Literature. I had completely bombed. And to get into Borough Road and achieve my desired escape I needed at least two reasonably respectable grades.

The escape that I had been looking forward to, to moving on with my life, away from my broken heart and broken home, to starting to realise my dreams in a world beyond the one I felt trapped in, had not materialised. I sunk into a pretty deep level of despair, vin rouge and Gauloises, my favourite French cigarettes. My thoughts became really quite dark. I remember vividly thinking of suicide. Not of how or when, or what, or of it as a reality, but that word came into my head even if it left it as quickly. It was a disconcerting place to find myself in.

My decision was to retake the A levels I had flunked. A sheer determination and stubbornness to be able to take up that place at the college of my choice, just a year later than planned, set in. Determination can be a positive trait. It can also have more negative consequences. Term time came around. Bored by only having a couple of classes to attend a week my only real distraction was playing hockey for school, town and county. I got an evening job in a pub to occupy some of my time, my mind and energy. My greatest confidante, who had broken my heart, wrote regularly to me from the place she had escaped to. Her success in getting away and changing her life seemed only to exacerbate my own sorry situation.

Timeframes are slightly muddied here. Mum and I were living in the old family home (I had returned to live with her after several years finding no way out of a difficult time living with Dad). This previously magnificent home steeped in a rich heritage and much laughter and many happy memories, was now a shadow of where I had grown up. We couldn't afford more than the one gas heater which we moved from room to room in the vast space, depending on where we were spending our time. We held hall sales to sell off toys to make some money. And I kept all of my troubles to myself, as I know my mother did hers.

At some stage, I started taking laxatives. I will not indulge you with any detail but my circumstances were taking me into the world of an eating disorder. I have no recollection of why I started on this route. I don't recall having an especially poor body image. It may have been about control. I believe it most certainly would have been to do with self-respect, self-esteem and the feeling of failure and lack of validation. Those things are probably enough. As time went on (I would say about 4 to 5 months) I was losing some weight. Mum and I moved to a small townhouse, which was a good thing, and she was by now spending increasing amounts of time with a family friend whose wife had died. He told me about a small health club that he went to and encouraged me to try it out. I did. And became obsessive about exercise. And started to lose furious amounts of weight. The irony is that I felt fit. I felt healthy. I felt satisfied and I did feel in control. And confident. But I went from 10.5 to 7 stone within a matter of months. I was eating very healthily when I ate. But I was punishing my body with the amount of exercise I was doing in the gym, walking, running. My stepfather-to-be virtually moved in with us and was the only person I recollect addressing my anorexia/exercise bulimia with me. One evening he and I were sitting watching TV, he recumbent on the floor as was his way, me curled up in an armchair. Mum wasn't in the room. Without making eye contact he said this to me, "You know if you don't start eating more you won't have the energy to go on tour to Germany. What a pity that would be. I'm just saying." I didn't reply, we continued with our eyes focused on the TV and no more was said. I was due to go away with the county hockey team in a few months' time. This was something so important to me and I would deem it a failure if I wasn't able to go. Things had switched for me in that moment.

I went on that hockey tour. That summer we all moved to a beautiful home together outside Burton. Mum married and I gained a stepfather. And having risen to 8 stone in September of 1978, I took up my place at Borough Road College.

I maintained my friendship, albeit from afar, with the woman who had perhaps kick started a series of events. I returned to boyfriends at college in my first 2 years. As I went away, she returned home. Throughout our mid to late 20s, we remained good friends with me visiting her and she visiting me in London, coming into what was by then my clearly gay existence. Whatever had passed back in our late teens was never spoken of. We carried on exchanging Christmas cards until recent years, and then they arrived no longer.

It was the first cut. More were to come for me in the ensuing years but that was the deepest, most revealing and most damaging. The repercussions of which, although not by choice, have likely remained with me.

Us . . .

Poncy places
Funny faces
Common phrases
Feisty phases
Funky, inhibited, cowed
Spunky, spirited, proud.

My Family and Other Beings

We have so many different relationships. One of the longest standing relationships in my life with any man has been with my hairdresser. Throughout moves to different ends of the country, illness and other obstacles, we have pretty much managed to collide in London every few months for over 20 years in order that he can cut, colour and finger-dry me to my satisfaction.

I have two nieces who are the best any aunt could ask for. Clever, kind, funny, and with whom I enjoy time as friends and confidantes when necessary.

In 2015, I was delighted to be asked to be godmother to the daughter of one of my oldest friends. A first for me and something that I had longed for and felt sad to have previously missed out on. Although still very young, my goddaughter has enchanted me with her charm, character and presence of mind.

One of my own godmothers, also my aunt, became a friend and confidante in my life and when she died a few years ago, it was with great sadness but in celebration of her memory that I wrote this letter to my cousins.

Friday, June 22nd 2012.

Forgive me for typing this letter but Marg thinks my writing is quite hard to read although I don't know what she can mean!

This morning finds me feeling very sad and blubby after receiving your message about Auntie's passing. I am so very sorry to hear this – for her and for you and for all of us – I simply adored her and am naturally thinking of you all so much today.

What can I say about Auntie?

A stunning, remarkable, extraordinary, adorable individual!

Someone who was faced with immense challenges but who always rose to the occasion.

Someone who was at times naughty, outspoken, outrageous, but who pretty much always and rightly managed to get away with it. I think of her driving me to a restaurant once years ago applying her lipstick as she swung round hairpin bends – marvellous.

Someone with "largesse" in a world where that often seems to have gone out of fashion. Her kindness, warmth, generosity of spirit and determination always shone through. Thirteen years ago she somehow managed and manipulated her way to my 40th birthday party in London. Even with her limited mobility, she got herself by train to Canterbury, hijacked her poor friend and made her drive them up to Brixton and back, all in the same evening so that she could be there to celebrate with me! How chuffed was I … and appreciative.

Like naughty schoolgirls we shared tales, troubles, too much wine, too many fags!! She was interested in me and I in her, recognising in each I think, a kindred spirit. Let's face it neither of us ever chose to be too conventional and didn't really like to do what we were told!

And finally, and above all she made me laugh. So easily, so often and so much. With her funny faces, her wicked and witty asides, her actions which sometimes demonstrated her vulnerability, as well as her ability to laugh at herself. When she was looking after me as a youthful 22-year-old at your home in Manorbier, post glandular fever, there came a knock at my door late one night. In walked a vision that was my dear Aunt – torn stockings, bruised arms, looking bedraggled and very sorry for herself. "You won't bloody believe what just happened to me," she wailed…" No…", I chuckled. "I fell in the pond!" No-one could have fitted more snugly into that pond than Auntie – it was made for her!! Boy did we laugh that night.

So to end my ramble…

She was your Mum.

She was my Auntie, my Godmother, my mate. She may be gone but oh brother she will never be forgotten!

That woman was at times the funniest person. She was a friend and someone I felt able to talk openly to about my own vulnerabilities and dreams. She did likewise, and it was wonderful to experience. She was very fond of lipstick and I delighted myself and I hope her by throwing my Chanel lippy on top of her coffin just in the nick of time before the soil landed on top of it. She had better have made good use of it.

D

Disrespectful

Disingenuous

Dishonest

Disappointing

Dismissive

Damaging

Deceitful

Devastating

Duped

Denied

Done over

Ddddddddd

Don't know why

Don't understand

Didn't have to be that way

Angry-you damn well better believe it

Forgive and forget-you darn well have to be joking

I'm done

Family Secrets. Interview. Original interview conducted by Jo Morris. Woman's Hour. 31 January 2019.

I have taken the questions from that interview as asked by Jo but have replaced the answers with my own.

1. So tell me a little bit about your family set up.

Until the age of 13 I lived with my Mum, Dad and two older sisters in a large house in a square with a church at its centre where my mother and my maternal grandfather had also been brought up. My maternal grandparents lived downstairs, we lived upstairs in the house that had been separated horizontally. There were a lot of other relatives who lived around the same square and nearby.

2. What is/was your relationship like with your Mum and Dad?

I don't remember having an unusual relationship with my parents as a child. Once my parents split up, the relationship with my father became very fractious, with my mother stronger. Although we haven't always talked or shared confidences, my mother and I have always looked out for each other. This was not the case with my father. As I grew up it remained a cautious relationship, until I was in my 50s when it became respectful and very loving. Sadly, this has been negatively affected by circumstances in the last few years.

3. So you discovered a family secret and kept that secret.

One Sunday afternoon when I was 12, there was a large family gathering for afternoon tea downstairs with my grandmother. A visiting aunt asked, "So girls, you must be every excited about Dad's new house?" My middle sister and I exchanged bemused looks and my sister suggested that I go to the kitchen where mum was making a fresh pot of tea to ask her about this revelation. Looking stunned Mum sat me on a stool at the kitchen table, placing her hands on my shoulders. What she had to share with me was that she had been having an affair with a family friend (I will refer to him as "Uncle"), and that she and Dad would be splitting up, that she and "Uncle" would eventually be setting up home together and indeed Dad was buying a new house. "Could you keep this a secret from your middle sister for now?" she asked. My sister had a mock O level coming up and it would be better if she didn't know just yet. I remember my Mum crying as her truths unfolded. I do not remember whether I did. I have no recollection what I said when I returned to my grandmother's lounge and a fresh cup of tea.

Gradually things dawned on me. Little things I had noticed that hadn't seemed odd at the time. Mum kissing 'Uncle" at the bottom of the stairs in a way that was unusual for friends. Mum and Dad suddenly having single beds in their bedroom. Dad becoming very obstreperous when he had had a few drinks.

My parents were to split up the following year. I was 13 years old. It seems ironic because I recall being teased by my middle sister when we were young about not being able to keep secrets. I had kept one of the biggest secrets I would ever be expected to keep in my life.

4. Why didn't you ask your Mum more about it? Talk more about it.

I guess I feared what I might hear. It was a lot for a child to deal with. I think we all just got on with it and only confronted things as were forced upon us. Friends at school were in similar situations. Some told stories that seemed weird to me. My own situation seemed relatively calm and amicable. My parents didn't argue. Mum did tell me often that they had stayed together as long as they had because they thought it best if we were of an age where we could understand and to know each parent well, rather than being separated from one at a very young age. She always questioned whether that had been the right decision. I admired both of my parents for how they managed. There was still the broader family and everyone seemed to carry on as normal or close to it. I never once thought it was any fault of my own.

5. Were you protecting your middle sister? How did that affect you? How did you manage it when it came out? Who did you feel was responsible? Did you blame your Mum or your Dad?

I was definitely protecting my sister. I had been asked to. Sworn to secrecy. I don't remember when they told her or what impact that had. I was ahead of the game in trying to get my head and heart around it.

Mum was of course responsible for the act of having an affair, but I firmly believe that it takes two to tango and that there must have been weaknesses in Mum and Dad's relationship for the affair to happen and for it to continue.

6. How did you feel when it came out? A burden released?

I don't remember.

7. Where did the unravelling of this take the family?

Mum and Dad were steadfast in their devotion to trying to maintain good relations with each other and us. Initially, we all went to live with my dad in his new house on the other side of town. Mum would frequently come up for supper and I would spend my weekends with her. The affair she had didn't last much longer. It turned out that the man she had given up so much for, and with whom she was already creating a home, had been double crossing her. Her life was in ruins. Her marriage over. Her daughters living with their father. Her mother aged and disabled. No source of income. In time, she was to remarry but not for many years. My father too. I lived with him for four years until our fighting was too much for everyone. I returned to live with my wounded but resilient mother.

8. How is the relationship with your Mum, Dad? Sisters? What happened to the affair that broke the family up? Has that come back to haunt you?

Both of my parents are still alive as I write. Mum is 92 and living in a care home near our hometown. She has dementia but remains resilient and I visit her every couple of months, spending several days with her. She has no real conversation but still cares and retains a great sense of humour. Dad is 97 and lives in a nursing home in north Wales not far from the home he lived in with my stepmother. I have not seen him for one and a half years. Circumstances arose a few years ago that I lived with for some time, until I felt that for the sake of my health I should distance myself. I write to him occasionally. He always enjoyed my "chatty" letters and complimented me on my writing. I hope to go and see him in the summer when I feel free to do so again.

Dad has always been very supportive of Mum. For him "Uncle" was the bad guy, commonly referred to as "the shit", especially after he had unceremoniously dumped my Mother. Fair enough really. My own regard for that person was more complicated.

Mum once said to me, "You can never trust a soul." I don't agree with that, but I think it did throw up trust issues. But it was a learning experience. You come to understand people, their emotions, that they do bad things. But that respect and tolerance are critical to getting by with people. We weren't a family keen on openness or frank discussions. We seemed to keep our emotions in check and go about our lives in our own, very different ways. For most of my young adulthood I questioned in my own mind who my Dad was. I didn't feel able to cry openly until I was at college and a friend encouraged me to. My first counselling sessions in a way.

My relationship with my sisters has changed and evolved over the years. I maintain that despite the differences in our characters and lifestyles we used to muddle along very well. As a small child, my eldest sister had my back. As an adult, I became good mates with my middle sister and we were there for each other. On one occasion when we had had quite a lot of wine we even tried to track "Uncle" down to no avail. I guess we wanted as adults to confront him.

My Dad and Me

Marg and I are seated either side of the long dining table in my father's home in north Wales. The house is perched at the top of a steep and meandering slope (Angina Hill as it was more commonly known) overlooking the sweeping and picturesque Abersoch Bay. It is a lovely, balmy May evening in 2013. Boats bobbing on the sea. The sound of the odd jet ski circling the sea for a last gasp run out for the day. Gulls swooping around the telegraph wires lining the lane down. Below and cut off from the beach by the luxuriant dunes, golfers slowly make their way round their last few holes relishing the early summer evening sunshine. Dad holds court at the end of the table. We have bought a takeaway curry for supper. A long-time favourite. Along with meringues, creamy puddings of any description, and Galaxy bars. And red wine. Well wine of any colour. He is 91. His wife, my stepmother, is in hospital, a frequent but at that time, not serious occurrence. Dad is considering the remains of the feast in front of him and whether he can squeeze anymore in. He eyes something.

"I think I've had enough, really."

"There's some lamb there."

"Oh, shut up. I'll go on eating and eating."

"Last time, a month ago when we had a curry, you had two enormous platefuls," I point out.

"Doesn't mean you have to tonight though! Don't feel we're forcing you."

He would have gone on eating but time intervened. It was nearly 9pm and his attention turned to other things. "I've got two minutes and I take my tablets and then bugger everything. I've got sleeping tablets and one's for my leg if I get the cramp. It is bloody awful." He is referring of course to the vagaries of age.

Belly laughs abound. He is a funny man. He has a great sense of humour even if at times it verges on the bawdy and politically incorrect. He has a wonderful ability to make people laugh. He is also a gentle man in both senses of the word. Gentleman Johnny he used to be called. Always well turned out, impeccable manners, well-meaning and generous to a fault. A believer in the goodness of people and very trusting in humanity. And a man staggeringly self-aware for his generation and happy in his older years to share his thoughts and opinions about himself.

His love affair with curry and all things from the Indian continent are a throwback to his time in the army after the Second World War. Generally, after most meals, where there was more than one drink involved, he would regale us with tales of his first love, warmly recollecting his time in India and with her. I have a great many of his photographs from those times. Dapper Dad standing proudly in his khakis, more often than not as was to be the case throughout his life when the sun was warm enough with his top off, pipe in his mouth. Back then a sharp moustache too. Slim, fit, handsome and although having a natural propensity to look rather serious, when smiling – the twinkliest of eyes. Something he has never lost.

As a GP in Burton upon Trent he maintained his affinity with India and Pakistan through his patients, insisting that their homes were cleaner than any others and enjoying buying spices from their small neighbourhood shops close to his surgery. He was a very proficient cook.

When a drink had loosened his tongue, Dad's self-awareness would be revealed. This was when he felt able to reflect freely about his life and what had formed him. Even referring on one occasion to the time when he was due to be dispatched to foreign lands as an army officer. "I went to see my CO and told him that I didn't want to be sent to the Far East. That those places would be too hostile for me and I didn't think I was strong enough to cope there. I had an inferiority complex you see. And bless him he took that on board and sent me instead to Egypt and India."

An amazingly frank admittance. Not only for him to share with me, but with his commanding officer back in the 1940s. It would be a courageous request to make even in today's more forgiving times. Even more so then. In equal measure, it was a mark of the CO himself that he respected my father's wishes.

I have been intrigued by this lack of confidence and "inferiority complex" for a long time. There was nothing in my father's background to encourage him towards it other than a domineering mother who I imagine he obeyed at every turn. Dad always deferred to other people, more often than not the women in his life, believing, trusting perhaps that they knew better. That they were doing right by him when it wasn't really what he wanted. He wanted to be an architect and had an immense talent for drawing and making things, such as flat-pack Wendy houses for my nieces, speedboats for himself, all without any plans or ready-made designs. His mother wanted him to be a doctor so that's what he did. She thought it was socially more advanced than being an architect, although I'm not sure why. This lack of confidence to challenge his own beliefs about himself manifested when my mother engaged in an affair that was to ultimately break up our family. When talking to Marg and I that same evening, about his friend, who subsequently let my mother down, he said "I was boring. I wasn't a great person at going out other than to the tennis club to get whistled. I think your Mum wanted something better than that, so she got close to that man. Well fair enough, he opened the world to me. He took me all sorts of places." Philosophical, generous towards the person who changed his world and that of our whole family. Of course, in cases of marital breakdown both parties generally need to take some responsibility for allowing it to happen. But Dad was effectively blaming himself still, 40 years later.

This self-reflection touched me in a very personal way when, in the summer of 2017 on one of my trips to see him, by then in a nursing home, he started musing. "I've been a useless father to you. You've achieved so much and with no help from me." I wasn't able to comment. I knew that he admired my writing, if only from the chatty letters I had sent him over recent years. When I brought out my first album, he was very sad that due to his very poor hearing he has never heard it and won't be able to hear other music of mine. A sadness I shared. He was right to a degree about his abilities as a father to me. I'm not sure he knew to how much of an extent. Whether he was referring to times gone by or more recent circumstances. Perhaps to all of them. He was, after all such a self-aware man. More likely that he just couldn't confront it.

Were these musings a form of apology? Feelings of remorse? It was an acknowledgment of sorts, but he didn't actually say that he was sorry for having been a poor father or why he thought he was. I see so many friends and relatives of my own generation bringing their children up with such awareness, sensibility and such incredibly high levels of engagement and I know that many of my peers, including myself, didn't experience that. I believe this is a characteristic of the times we were brought up in. I hope that in time, if we have time, I can continue that conversation with him. I think of him a lot and I sense that he probably does likewise. He is a thinking man. If he gets to read this book I hope that he will take the tales I tell in the heartfelt and warm way that they are intended. They are just honest thoughts and feelings. Not intended to be hurtful or shocking. Just open.

As I write this, Dad is now 97 and still living in the nursing home in north Wales. My stepmother died 2 years after that curry evening and it was no longer possible for my father to live alone. A lot of water has passed under the bridge since her death. My stepmother was a big influence in all aspects of my gentle and generous natured Dad's life. In the vacuum after her death, influence was contested, loyalties shifted, family dynamics changed. Opportunities that might have been freed up for me to nurture our relationship more, to help care for him, have been made difficult and become fewer. And I have grieved. I have a great deal of love and affection for my Dad. I hope he still has for me.

I have continued as much as possible to visit him. Over the last 18 months I haven't in order to distance myself from things that have become too painful. Time takes its toll on us all. I no longer get to visit his house in that very special spot overlooking Abersoch Bay. It is still there but has been passed on to another family member and staying there is not an option. He can no longer eat curries but does occasionally get to eat a meringue, which I make sure I take for him when I make the long journey up to visit. He no longer gets to drink wine. I do that for him instead. I like my dad. I believe he likes me. And loves me. I have always and will always love him to bits.

Why don't you ever ask
Why don't you understand
Why don't you ever ask
Why don't you understand.

Why

Travel

Caribbean Queens

In 1998, Marg and I ventured to the Caribbean and a double destination trip taking in Cuba, heavenly Havana being our favourite place. I simply adore the rugged, ancient, colonial architecture. The old cigar factory, and the beautiful ballet dancers working their magic in their none too splendid surrounds, now modernised by the brilliant Carlos de Acosta. Belize was part two of this trip. Outdoor pursuits. In a group. Teamwork I like, group activities I'm not so keen on. Cycling in the searing midday sunshine. Not just mad dogs and Englishmen but in my mind, a negligent travel company too, with fellow travellers dropping like flies that day. Next was hiking. I dropped out before it started. It was far too ambitious for me. Then we got taken by boat, out of the reef across open water, to a true Robinson Crusoe island owned by the company. We slept in bamboo huts with rush roofs set on stilts. Some dived. Some lazed around. Some snorkelled. It was stunning. And never more so than when the day came for us to leave. The day before, we had found out that the weather was going to be challenging. On the morning of departure, we were prepped over breakfast – a bunch of about twelve of us. Some with more bravado and arrogance than I had thought was humanly possible, some sitting quietly. There had been storms the previous night and the seas would be high. A boat was due, bringing a new group in and we would be leaving on that. We were advised to take a sea sickness pill and told to wear our life jackets. The boat appeared, emerging gingerly across the water. And docked. Two people were carried off which didn't fill us with confidence. We carefully climbed aboard, all asked to sit astern. The very experienced captain's nervousness was palpable. He had to negotiate his way through the low water without running aground. The seas ahead were high and pretty perilous. We sat in complete silence, some I imagine saying silent prayers, huddled together, Marg and I holding hands, knuckles white. I wasn't capable of speech.

The Caribbean featured in two other holidays. Grenada to see mates who had moved there, including a short flight over to Trinidad to see old family friends. And Jamaica. Oh Jamaica! Definitely in my top five. We stayed at the trendy and bohemian Jakes Hotel on the wonderfully named Treasure Beach, owned by the Henzell family. Perry Henzell is renowned for making the film *The Harder They Come*. Small rustic rooms with open air showers, not en suite shower rooms here. A bathing hole amongst the rocks, and the deadliest and most delicious cocktails served up in the wooden shack out front.

From there we moved up into the Blue Mountains and the magnificent Strawberry Hill, owned by Chris Blackwell, the founder of Island Records. Style that was both simple but spectacular. Vertiginous verandas dangling as if from heaven on the edge of the rooms perched on the verdant mountainside, where fresh juices and breads were brought to us each morning as we lounged in our white, fluffy gowns amid the subtly designed dark wood and white linen surrounds, the sound of the hummingbirds trills greeting our ears.

And finally, to Jamaica Inn. Upgraded to a beach front suite, with private terrace overlooking the gardens, fronting the white sand where we would lie each morning. On the dot of 11am a waiter would invite us to take a rum punch. Glamour at its height. Probably the closest I'll ever come to the experience my mum had on her *Queen Mary* trip. Frequented in its day by Marlene Dietrich, Winston Churchill et al.

Perhaps the most significant day of this entire holiday was when we visited Firefly, the home of one of my heroes, Noel Coward, now a museum sitting up high with views over the island below and the gleaming Caribbean ahead. And then, having made prior contact with the owners, we paid a visit to the private and smaller residence that Mr Coward used for himself down amongst the rocks below, and which I had dreamt of renting for a significant birthday. We were welcomed and shown round this place where time seemed to have stood still. We never did get to rent it for any significant events, but it was an honour to have been given exclusive access to it. Noel Coward captivated my imagination from a young age. His flamboyance, his wit, his style, his way with words. He truly was The Master.

Music

There is a woman sitting on a train on her way back to Kent from London. She is looking out of the window at the unseasonably bright and warm February sunshine. She is reflecting on a love affair, a relationship she has had since she was a child. There is a warm glow about her. A gentle and satisfied smile crosses her face as her black painted nails tap gently on her knee. She wonders how it all came to this.

As she nears 60, she questions where this love will take her. For so much of her life she kept it hidden, her own secret passion, but for a few souls who she unknowingly let into her secret. Only a few of those encouraged her to bring her secret out into the open, to be not ashamed of it, but proud.

Her first love was, until she reached the age of 50, comparable to lust, an unattainable entity, something beyond her reach that existed only in her fantasies.

Now, 10 years later, and despite the many life changing obstacles, she is deeply ensconced in a steady relationship with the love that once dare not speak its name. She has allowed herself to take control, have confidence in it and feel worthy of it. She knows that whatever concerns she may have that it could all end tomorrow, the adventure she has been on already has been well worth the risks. It has all been worth it to gamble against her fears of rejection, to declare herself and dive naked into the sea of love that is music.

A girl who wanted so much to just sing, but who never felt brave enough, has become a woman. The train is returning her home from an afternoon spent at the iconic Abbey Road Studios where her second album of eight, self-penned songs and her own cover version of two others by favourite female artists, has just been mastered. This is the stuff of dreams. The smile turns into a grin.

A lifelong Beatles fan, since it was the Fab Four who made that place so famous, she felt no shame having her photograph taken walking across that zebra crossing nor when scrawling "The Window to My Soul. Mastered here 27/2/19, Jude" on the graffiti wall in front of the building.

She had always believed she could sing but only ever did so behind closed doors. Maybe there were a couple of occasions when, as a small child she stood with her cousins, belting out the hits of the day whilst wearing a hard, plastic Beatles wig.

But as she got older, whilst her friends joined choirs, she would content herself with providing vocal accompaniment to Dusty, the Fab Four, the Carpenters, Fleetwood Mac and Cat Stephens in the confines of her bedroom. The fun and games had turned into something more serious.

In his book, *Voices*, journalist Nick Coleman talks about how for some people, music is a very private experience and for others it is one to be shared. For her it was the former. A refuge from the turbulence of adolescence and an outlet for creativity and emotions.

So what got in the way?

My family knew that I loved pop music, but didn't most teenagers? Mine wasn't a musical family and I don't recall if they ever commented on my voice. I didn't have any desire to join a choir, which was the main way to express yourself musically at that time. I thought that everyone else would always be better than me. That to sing in public I had to be better than I was. People would judge me. I would experience rejection. To climb over that barrier just felt like it would bring home my worst fear – the fear of failing at the thing I loved to do more than anything in the world.

So that was that. I grew up, left home, continued enjoying music but sat on the sidelines in admiration whilst friends at college and beyond strummed their guitars and offered up their renditions of Madonna's song "Holiday".

Various partners along the way put up with late night, often alcohol-fuelled warblings. Sometimes I would let slip a carefully carried tune when in company and a friend might whip out their guitar and try and coax me into sharing a song. But still my singing remained private and largely hidden.

And then I met Marg. She bought me singing lessons. I didn't go. She believed in and respected me and my voice and encouraged me to do something with it. But age had stolen any confidence I had and my ambitions to one day sing in public, felt an insurmountable challenge.

Marg and I then moved from London to Kent. I continued to sing into the early hours in sessions we referred to as "buzzing". My own high. And then things came to a head. One night on holiday Marg took me to task.

"I'm getting fed up. You are going to have to tackle this. I don't want you to get to be 90 and turn to me and say 'I always knew I could sing but no one else did. Woe is me.' You're about to hit 50 – it's now or never!"

Tough love can be hard to hear, but that talking to was a critical turning point.

When we got home, Marg sought out several singing teachers and made me contact them. I found my match. Marg bought me a course of lessons and this time I went. I spent several months preparing, with the express aim of being able to sing at my 50th birthday party. Six months later I found myself on a stage, with a group of session musicians, performing in front of 100 unsuspecting friends and family. No rehearsals. No lyrics in front of me, (possibly the only time I have ever felt able to sing without my music stand and lyrics). They may not have been my songs, but it was my voice, me singing, and it was in public. It was a bit of a blur, supported by some champagne, cigarettes and diazepam but I had done it. I felt a groundswell of elation and sense of achievement beyond words. I had finally made it out from behind those closed doors. Could this passion, which had now at last been consummated, be turned into a lasting relationship?

I continued to take lessons and attended a couple of jazz workshops in London. Then, in January 2010, I was invited by a friend, who had been at my 50th party, to perform at a charity event. It would still be covers with backing tracks, but it was a start.

Then it all had to stop. In late 2011, after nearly a year of health struggles, I was told I had M.E.– a complicated, chronic illness. The smallest, most seemingly trivial tasks became impossible. In every way, performing was going to be too demanding. I would be unreliable and even if I could do it on the night there would be payback afterwards.

This was a severe blow. Having waited so long I didn't know what the future held. Would I ever sing again? If so, in what capacity? My focus had to shift to my recovery.

One of the many things I was encouraged to do to help with the more emotional aspects of M.E., was to start writing a journal. When I had allowed myself time and space to write creatively before, I had enjoyed it, but I was too impatient to allow myself to indulge. I had received very good reviews for my writing as a child. Now it became part of my daily routine. My illness had given me permission. It would absorb me for hours. Through writing, I found a lot of peace.

And then I found that some of my thoughts and feelings were a little like poems or perhaps even song lyrics. Sometimes I would find myself humming a little tune to them. I started to record those into my phone. My very own musical doodles.

I kept up vocal training when I could. And now I set about learning as much as I could about songwriting including reading books, doing online courses, watching documentaries and the BBC Masterclasses, following Carole King's advice, "Write from the heart. Write what you feel. And yes you can." Sage words from one of the very best. In early 2014, feeling that I had shaped my material into real songs, I went to see a local musician and producer and was given some very sound advice. "Go and find yourself a good arranger."

My instinct told me there was a person I'd met at those jazz workshops 3 years before who would be a good match. But she was an established, extraordinary musician, and was surely out of my league?

I summoned up all the courage I could and, quietening down the doubts, I carefully composed a message and sent it through her website. I waited a week or more and heard nothing. I was encouraged by my M.E. counsellor to chase this up. "So, what are you going to do about this Jude?", she asked as we discussed my dilemma and fears about how I might confront this challenge, both of us chuckling, knowing that in some ways my fears were of my own making. "I will text her, that's what I'll do." I don't like phoning people but texting was an action I felt was manageable. So, I did it. She hadn't got my message. I composed another one. We met a few weeks later in May 2014 and agreed to work together.

In the autumn of 2015, a group of the most wonderful musicians gathered at Livingstone Studios in north London to record my music. I sat in for 2 of the 3 days and was blown away. There was the sheet music with my name sitting proudly underneath the titles and all of this amazing talent, more used to performing or recording with household names, playing my songs. I sat in stunned silence, a lump building in my throat.

A month later, I recorded my vocals. It took several weeks to complete. I had to draw on every last drop of my still pretty-limited capacity, physically, mentally, emotionally and vocally. By the end I was totally spent. I had been pushed beyond my limits. Take after take, the concentration required and standing for long periods of time all took their toll. On the last day of recording, during the lunchtime break, I was in a positively euphoric state. The afternoon passed and I was almost throwing my non-existent hat up into the air when my engineer spoke to me through my headphones from the control room next door. I was told that I would have to record "Turn On the Moon" again because it wasn't up to the standard of the others. I agreed. But my heart and hopes plummeted. The adrenaline that had carried me through had raced away. I was completely and utterly exhausted. Had I pushed my ambitions too high and too hard for my health? As Marg drove me home I sobbed almost non-stop. But we returned the following week to re-record that song and tidy up a couple of others. It became my favourite song on that album.

Over the next few months, the editing, mixing and mastering took place. This Girl, This Woman. My debut album. Ten original songs written and sung by me.

Never in my wildest dreams did I believe that I would ever be saying that.

"A good LP is a being. It has a life force, a history and a personality, just like you and me," said Iggy Pop. And as such both deserve more than to be consigned to a stockroom, or even a bedroom. I had come out of my bedroom and sung in public. I had given birth to the life force that is an LP. Having fantasised about singing in public, maybe one day recording, I had turned that fantasy into a reality and I now wanted to share it with others.

As the album was nearing completion in April 2016, plans were underway to release it. I hadn't performed again in public since my M.E. diagnosis in 2011 and still didn't feel ready to so Marg and I decided on a multi-media event; a platform to tell my story in person through an In Conversation, with an exhibition of the lyrics, a talking heads video installation and a live performance of some of the songs by an established singer.

Marg and I had set about researching how we might get some financial support for the launch. We were awarded an Arts Council England grant and the generosity of many people who gave to a successful crowdfunding campaign completed that part of the process.

This all sounds pretty straightforward but it wasn't. The whole process was gruelling and the crowdfunding put Marg and I and our relationship under huge strain. There were times when we had to seriously consider pulling the plug because the impact on my health was beginning to tell.

But we pulled it off. And what a night we had. Saturday, 10 September 2016.

I went on to recreate the Launch of This Girl, This Woman on a smaller scale in a series of soirées, at a number of Kent Arts Centres throughout 2017 culminating in the Canterbury Festival Umbrella in addition to performing at Pride, Canterbury. It felt good to have started performing again. I can't say that I gave the best vocal performances of my life but each one got stronger, my confidence increased and I enjoyed them.

What follows is a transcript of a conversation between Marg and myself. An exploration. A reflection on what had happened, what was happening, what I wanted to happen, my motivations. 15 January 2017.

M: (talking about parents and aunts) I feel for some of that generation, they were prevented from fulfilling potential in life - and then people internalise this expectation, and shut up shop too early. You know when you said you think about your dad not having the get up and go to come to London. There were lots of reasons of course. But it brings it home that fundamentally life is about you and doing what fulfils you and not because you want other people to think you're great.

J: It is about fulfilment.

M: As soon as you start to go into promoting what you do to others, so that they like it, which you have to do of course, and you want that, it is risky, you can lose your way.

J: I think that's the thing because it is all about marketing and working out how best to try and promote all of this - the story, the music … You kind of lose sight of why you're doing it and what it's all about. I was looking through all the scribblings of the different lyrics and I suddenly thought, "This is what it's all about. Or partly what it's all about because it's the craft and all the hard work, wanting to create those lovely songs," and at a very difficult time. So suddenly that puts things back into perspective a little bit. It's about my fulfilment.

M: You said to me, "Am I doing the right thing?" And I feel that if you hadn't have done it, your life would be less rich. Fundamentally this is making your life richer and more satisfying and fulfilling.

J: I have broken out of lots of comfort zones. Starting to sing at 50 was taking myself right out of my comfort zone and doing something that I had feared but so wanted to do. I was talking to someone the other day about an idea I had had and said, "It's just so unlikely". And she said, "Most of what you've done in the past few years has been unlikely!"

M: You've always had a really strong vision.

J: I think at the moment I am just in this phase where we're pulling a lot of things together to try to create opportunities to blitz the media and hopefully get a few hooks to allow me to share my story more freely, and my music of course. And I'm trying to set up opportunities to do that in person. We're also trusting that we're taking the right approach.

M: You're doing all the right things. You just have to keep doing what you're doing. One area you might want to think about now is that the interview at the launch was very much about your personal story. I think then in the next 18 months as you promote this album, you can still have that, but also talk more about the songs. For example, "Don't Judge Me No More", what's behind that?

J: I'm hoping that if I get the opportunity to be interviewed then people will dig and start to ask about the songs as well.

M: Even "Soaking" … that song is all about your enforced recovery. Having to let go, not being able to drive yourself anymore. Ultimately, your coming to terms with that different way of being. The story is engaging and amazing. But coming out with number two should be about the contents of your art and not the contents of you. It will become natural that promotion is not only about self. Actually, the self creates the art. So, the more you've been in your own headspace, it's you who created the music, the art, and the story is the source. When people start singing without telling me I always think "just tell me". I want to know what's behind the song.

Throughout this time my story gathered quite a lot of press interest, both nationally and locally. I gave a lot of interviews and was pleased with how it was received. Several of the songs were used for a documentary called Older Women Rock which I was immensely proud of, its focus being on breaking down the perceived barriers and perceptions associated with women as they move into their 50s and 60s.

Not long after the launch, I'd found myself unknowingly entering a new and exciting chapter in my quest to work out where music would take me. In November, 2016, I went to a songwriting conference in London. One seminar given by a young woman stood out for me. She spoke eloquently, honestly, reassuringly and knowledgeably and had a track record as a performer and songwriter. A few months later, I looked into the possibility of booking a few vocal training sessions with her.

I started travelling down to Brighton every few weeks for vocal sessions. "You don't need to have such high expectations of yourself, Jude. None of us will be as wonderful on stage as we may think we are singing in front of the mirror in our bedroom." A very clear message that was to finally dispel the myth of perfectionism for me. "Accept that it is fine to set the bar lower than you ideally want to. Make your goals small, realistic and manageable. If you are tired don't practice. You don't have to practice every day." All good sense and obvious you would think but not something that comes easily to someone who sets out thinking that she has got to be better than good enough and won't be good enough wherever the bar is set. Everything she said seemed to underplay what I was always trying to do. A real less is more approach. I liked it. It resonated with me.

I don't actually remember exactly when I decided I would make another album. Certainly, the idea to write a book had come about throughout the time I had started to give interviews and do In Conversations at my soirées. I then started developing the concept of combining a book and an album. A "memoir of sorts" and songs triggered by the stories in the book.

Having got stuck into the writing of both things in early summer 2018, I had to start thinking then about how the album would be produced. I toiled over different options as far as people were concerned, until in one session my Brighton-based musical mentor told me, "Jude you are overthinking this. You can produce it. I can hold your hand and I know plenty of people who would be a good match to help shape the songs. You may not speak the language of music, but I can interpret for you. You have done it once and you actually know far more about this process, what is needed than you give yourself credit for." I stared at her in disbelief. "Really? I don't know about that." But the seed was sewn. I walked out of that session and along the Brighton seafront with a serious spring in my step. I had found what I was doing next.

And so, it came about rather incredibly that I was to write and perform the songs and, allowing me creative control over the whole project, be the executive producer. One of my co-producers could play a lot of the instruments on the album and we would bring in other musicians too.

Marg and I agreed early on to self-fund this project. No more crowdfunding. We did apply for various grants but were turned down. And so, as with other things in life, you try again. As I write this we await the decisions. But an independently made album and an independently published book would be the outcome.

My approach to making The Window to My Soul has been much less academic than This Girl, This Woman. Before I had done online courses, read songwriting books, had 1-2-1 lessons with professionals to critique my works in progress and also attended songwriting workshops. This time I wouldn't do many, if any, of those things. The way I wrote the songs for that first album was very detailed. Very thought through. I analysed the construction of each song from its rhyming schemes and structural options plus the theories behind them. I paid attention to syllables and musical parts. It was an immense learning curve. I was now prepared to break some of the rules. This time I would trust my instincts and what I had already learnt.

I was letting these songs write themselves a little bit more. They mostly follow a conventional structure. In some cases, the lyrics are more poetic than others and more lengthy. There is more storytelling in some. I was happy to strip the lyrics right back on occasion and was satisfied with oohs and aahs and repetition. I didn't always feel it necessary to fill gaps. In doing so, I found enormous freedom of expression.

This Girl, This Woman

That's What the Whisky's For

Forever My Love

Soaking All the Blues Away
(Featuring Sarah Jane Morris)

Don't Judge Me No More

Brief Encounter

Turn On the Moon

Heavenly

You Do Me Good

Me and Mrs Peel

Supported using public funding by
ARTS COUNCIL
ENGLAND

LOTTERY FUNDED

Getting one album under my belt had increased my confidence. I was clear about the sound and quality I wanted, the degree of pressure I was prepared to put myself under.

I worked with a group of young musicians, something which delighted me. I am a defender to the end of older people and women especially, but I am not exclusive in that and have relished the chance to show that we can all work together. Nothing makes my heart rate soar more dangerously than hearing "new" talent referred to almost always as "young". I am fully supportive of young people, but please let's hear more from, and for, the innovative older members of society.

I can also say that at no stage did I feel that this was a notoriously difficult second album. We opted consciously for a more organic process as the demo tracks evolved and recording took place. I was made to stand on my own two feet as I relied upon my intuition, the feel of the songs and allowed myself to be assertive about what I wanted and believed was right. My two co-producers and I formed a tight, collaborative team. One of them, also my vocal coach and musical mentor, was there to nudge me gently along, I had an engineer and arranger who clearly relished working on this project. It was my album. I wrote the songs and sung the songs but we were all producing it and appearing on it. It was a comfortable, incredibly enjoyable and empowering experience. A total joy.

The woman who sat on a train returning home from London a week ago is now sitting on a sofa in her kitchen at home. She glances out of the window from time to time as she taps away on her computer. In a matter of weeks, she will have finished her book as well as her album. That will have been a learning curve not quite to match her first album but an undertaking that with hindsight she may have shied away from. Apart from all the less-than-romantic but necessary administrative and logistical elements that still have to take place, her job is nearly done. She will set them free in person and plans to give the performance of her life so far, a little over 10 years after she set foot on her first stage.

She is finally settled in a steady and long-term relationship with her love of music. The early disruptive stirrings and lust may have gone but it has matured into a real part of her life. Still unsure about where it will take her, but content that she is no longer an imposter in the world of music, she is worthy of her place and happy to let it take her by the hand and lead her where it will. She has also finally rediscovered the fun and games of music, just like the uninhibited child in a Beatles wig she once was.

To put things in perspective
It's curious to observe
That since you disappeared
I've rediscovered my nerve.

To Put Things in Perspective

Challenges with performing

I return to the issues that prevented me from singing in public when I was younger and to those that I have continued to experience more recently. Here I would like to delve a little more deeply into the challenges presented by performing. An exploration if you like.

What is it that I feel about singing? What is it that I experience? Why do I have any hesitations? What's the worst that can happen?

Performing isn't something that has ever come easily to me. I tend to be consumed for several days beforehand but once on stage I settle in for the ride. I liken this state to taking an exam. The build-up and anticipation is often harder than the event itself. Perhaps fear, perhaps excitement, or confusion? The adrenaline mounting only to find its release once the time arrives to perform.

And what happens when you've brought out an album? This was what faced me when I had brought out my first album. You can sit back and be satisfied. You can tour it. Performing had taken me way out of my comfort zone even before I was ill. It had taken me until I was 50 to find the courage to do it in the first place. Could I do it all over again? Would I have the capacity to and if so, when? Did I want to put myself through that? Would my experience be different? Was I prepared to take further risks, to gamble again on this love to see this time if I could make it last? I knew full well that you had to be prepared to get turned down and get up again when that happened. I continued to receive encouragement from those who recognised the desire in me and believed I had the ability to set my bar high. As long as I had the energy, I had the ambition and could achieve whatever I wanted to. It depends what it is you want and how far you are prepared to go to find it.

What was clear was that I would start performing a little again. I had decided to give it my best shot. I wanted to and thought I could.

I have also considered that I might not be a natural performer. But then perhaps I am? Perhaps being in the spotlight is not my natural place in life. Of that I wouldn't be certain. I could forget my lyrics. I could go wrong with the melody. I could be out of tune. Anyone accompanying me could go wrong. And in the realm of things what do those things matter? You can "wing" it. I have done that before. You could stop, make a joke which would go down well, shows you're human, fallible, and people enjoy that. I know I do. It happens to the best of performers. I have done that too. Although it's probably best not to make a habit of it.

I have written notes to myself to try and find reassurance as a show looms and when those feelings of fear and anticipation start to creep upon me. I have recited mantras. Taken medication, used meditation, cigarettes and alcohol. For so many people who perform in any capacity, they are putting themselves and their vulnerability on the line. Despite any degree of belief, they still experience huge self-doubt, the fear of rejection, solitude, the guilt of the selfishness that is required to do this thing, self-destructive impulses sometimes to express their art, and to overcome the fear of exposing themselves to judgement and criticism.

Without performing regularly, I have effectively been redundant and inactive as a singer until a few weeks before a gig, which was when I would get into practice mode. Very little singing would have otherwise taken place. So, unlike the years of my youth when singing was private and largely closeted, unlike the subsequent years when the late night "buzzes" took place, I found myself in a relative dearth, where singing and music played a very small part in my life until another performance was on the horizon.

I am not a professional musician and would therefore find it necessary, as I almost always have done, to host my own events. And with that comes a cost. I neither have the capacity nor the desire to do pub gigs or be part of a function band so my opportunities are limited. It is very, very hard out there even for established, professional musicians. Making a living out of music is a tough existence. Both live with venues closing down, or not paying out, with audiences reluctant to pay for creativity. And in the case of recorded music, the advent of downloading and streaming has hit the pocket of musicians badly. I read recently of a very experienced and established musician who was part of quite an influential band in the 70s and 80s who still perform. A well-known song of theirs that has been downloaded over 25,000 times had earned him 77p.

In the run up to recording, my singing is cranked up to whip the voice into shape, to practice the songs. Daily exercises involve a routine for breathing and vocal health but overall the amount of time I spend singing is a real case of feast or famine. I would like that to change and am not satisfied that that is the way things will always be from now on. I will be exploring some more innovative ways of making that change possible, manageable and viable.

I believed that I could do all of this and I believe I will find ways that suit me to continue with my musical adventure for a long time to come.

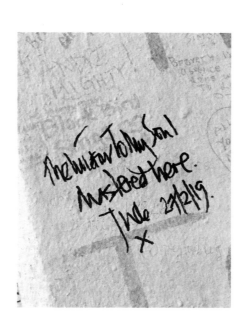

Travel

The Marrakesh Express

When you read this, will have made our sixth trip to Morocco, mixing it up amongst the minarets and the largest urban car free medina in the world that is Fes, and back to our beloved and magical Essaouria, where we will have sat atop the roofs on the terrace of our apartment. Listening to the hubbub of gentle hypnotic music, workers going about their business, the laughter of children, a moped here, gulls there. Then every few hours the call of prayer echoing around the medina. The sun casting shadows across the tiled walls. Wood smoke wafting through the air from the chimneys. Gently sipping fresh ginger tea to nurse our obligatory fragile stomachs. The warmth of the sun and tender breeze nurturing us through and through. A hammam where I get water thrown over me, black soap rubbed into me, and am scoured and pummelled almost to oblivion. I love them. It will have been our fifth time holidaying in Essaouria and one might wonder why we considered returning even for a second time given what I am about to tell you.

Our most spectacular Moroccan trip was our own version of the Marrakesh Express in the winter of 2007. Martha Gelhorn would doubtless have included this in her *Journeys from Hell*.

There is something magical in the air in Essaouria and as with most places I would recommend you go and experience it for yourself. Our first visit was in the December of that year. We had planned our journey meticulously, leaving home in Kent and going by Eurostar to Paris. Having been there a few times, we would only stay in Paris for an afternoon before going on to Madrid by sleeper train where we would have a whole day. Then another train to Algeciras, a night in a hotel and across to Tangiers on a morning hydrofoil where we would spend a day before getting another overnight train to Marrakesh and a car to Essaouria to spend a week sunning ourselves, recovering, revelling in the romance of the journey we had just undertaken.

But it didn't quite work out like that. This was the December when snow stopped play. And Eurostars. We only realised a day or two before that there were likely to be cancellations on the first stage of our journey. But with the enterprising support of friends, we secured first class tickets on a ferry crossing from Dover to Calais after a short train journey from home. Dover Ferry Terminal was like a cattle market, with thousands of people fighting to find tickets to get to wherever home was for Christmas. Once in Calais we had to walk through knee-deep snow with our trolley bags to a hotel we had had the foresight to book. We were accompanied in our sorry little gang of waifs and strays by a father and son trying to get home to Israel. I hope they made it. Our travel plans already gone awry but confident we could get them back on track the next morning, we got a train to Paris, crossed the city of love to leave our bags at Gare d'Austerlitz Station, returning early evening to board our 8pm train to the Spanish capital. By which time, I was feeling rather queasy. We waited. And waited. Only to be told that we would have to travel to Tours by coach as there had been a derailment. We eventually left around 11pm. I held onto my stomach and hoped very much for the best, the toilets in the coach being out of service. We got to Tours and transferred on to our sleeper train. It duly arrived in Madrid on the appointed morning but several hours later than scheduled. We dashed off to the Museo Reina Sofia to see Picasso's Guernica, one of the main reasons for choosing a stop off in Madrid, only to find it closed. Warning: many places close on a Monday. Do not make plans for a Monday when travelling. We hopped over to the Prado for a brief look and to fulfil our tradition of buying mugs in foreign museums and gave in to a desire to spend the remainder of the afternoon eating tapas and downing Rioja. Then we went back to the railway station to collect our bags and catch our train, for half of our journey, until we had to get off and pick up a coach on to Algeciras. We stayed the night in Spanish splendour in a Moorish hotel and after breakfast the next day, casually decided to go off for a stroll. Whilst out we thought we would pop in and pick up our hydrofoil tickets. And were told that it wasn't running because the sea was too rough. Instead we could get a ferry but in 30 minutes. We made our way back to the hotel by taxi to pick up our luggage, settle up and get back for the boat and onwards across the sea to Morocco. We made it in time and then had the pleasure of trying determinedly to play Scrabble on the top deck where there was some fresh air, despite our feet being suspended off the floor to avoid the carpet of seawater and vomit swishing beneath us. We made it to Tangiers where it was pouring with rain and had to disembark from the car deck as it wasn't safe to use the pedestrian exit. We walked off, along with the cars, lugging our trolley bags once again behind us to find out that we were supposed to have had our passports stamped on the boat, on the 4th floor. By this time my stress levels were becoming quite extreme, so Marg took the risk of taking both passports up on her own. When the going gets tough and maybe feels tougher for one, the other steps up and carries a bit more of the load. She could, after all, also negotiate in French. I remained on the boat and watched in wonder as cars and passengers loaded on to the car deck for the return voyage. We made it off the ferry, somehow with passports stamped despite me not being present, just in time before the horn sounded and the ferry slipped out of the harbour. What Marg also chose not to tell me and that the officials had ignored, was that in fact my passport was out of date.

We chose an afternoon drinking gin in the El Minzah Hotel, rather than go sightseeing in the extraordinarily unseasonal downpour. We then caught our sleeper train to Marrakesh, followed by a taxi on to Essaouria where I spent much of our week being ill. The weather was inclement to say the least. On arriving we were met by quite biblical scenes: bridges down, the beach strewn with debris of all kinds. And in the midst of the midden that our holiday had become, I heard on Christmas Day that an aunt had died. An aunt I had grown up with along with the many relatives that surrounded us throughout childhood and beyond. Someone in whose home I had spent so many happy hours growing up.

Can you ever return
They don't know how beautiful it be.
Can you ever return.
They don't know how good you are for me.

Second Time Around

Travel

Outro

I am nearing the end of my travelling tales now. All of my tales in fact. It has been almost 2 weeks since we got back from the music festival in Flo. No red flags have appeared as yet on our globe. No further mention has been made of year-long camper van trips across Europe. I have just recovered from a week in one. Wimbledon is still on. England have been knocked out of the football World Cup but covered themselves in glory doing so. I have finished the Martha Gelhorn book. It was published in 1978, a full 40 years ago. She brings her stories to an end by making mention of the ease with which travel has become so accessible to so many, even, "football fans in yelling hordes follow their teams from country to country". She nor I would have believed back then that they would be able to do so to Russia with the ease with which they have this summer. She speaks deliberately negatively of the pitfalls of travelling because that fulfils the purpose of her book. Whether it be what we may experience when we are away, or those we encounter trying to get to where we are going. But I will end with her final words because ultimately, I believe the opportunity to travel and the opportunities it brings, to be a truly wonderful thing. To be able to. To feel the thrill of leaving home for a short or long time and to returning. Going to places close by or to foreign lands, the sense of adventure. This is why we will keep on doing it.

"Our hearts are light and gay because now it's happening, we're starting, we're travelling again."

I hope to keep starting, to keep it happening, to keep travelling again and again as I wend my way through my life wherever it takes me from here on in.

Bonus Track

The House Fast Asleep

The stillness of the night.
A house so fast asleep.
It holds its breath, afraid to be heard.
Afraid to make a peep.

Do I flush the loo if I have to go?
Will the walls open their eyes and stare?
Gasp in wonder, give me funny looks,
What the hell, do I really care?

Acknowledgements

Marg Mayne. My wife, best friend, partner and the greatest giver of love and support.

Marnie Summerfield-Smith. Editor and mentor. For her reassurance and encouragement. For coaxing me into giving just a little bit more at every turn.

Bob Carling. For being my advisor and guide through the minefield that is self publication and distribution.

Jane Ward and Klaudyna Walkowicz. Parkers Print and Design. For your time, talents and patience.

Lisa Smith, Nutritionist. www.nutriology.co.uk. and

Ashok Gupta, Founder of the Gupta Programme. www.guptaprogram.com. For their generosity, time, wise words and support.

Carly Vaughan. Graphic designer for front cover, author profile imagery and groovy fonts.

Lee Thompson. Photographer for author profile picture.

Jeremy Toynbee. Copy editor.

Emma Loft. Transcriber.

Ingram Sparks Publishing and Distribution.

All the amazing people I have been privileged to know in my life. Friends, acquaintances, partners, family. People I wished I had met. Anyone who has inspired or influenced any part of this book.

And to everyone who has bought this book and read any part of it.

I am truly grateful and thank you from the bottom of my heart.

Jude Adams.